IN THE BELLY OF THE SNAKE

West Africa over sixty years ago

Geoffrey Parrinder

CONTENTS

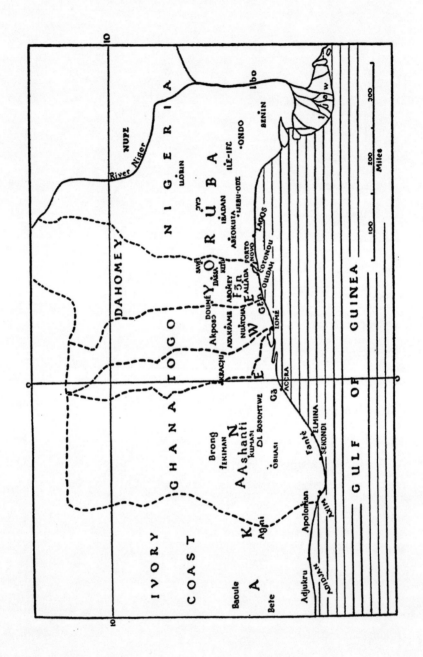

IN THE BELLY OF THE SNAKE

FOREWORD

To be asked to write a Foreword to a book by Geoffrey Parrinder is both an honour and a pleasure. I cannot, of course, lay claim to the depth of scholarship for which he has been rightly honoured. But in this case personal acquaintance during a time of ministry in Kent and knowledge of the area about which he writes may be more significant. For his house in Porto Novo was my home too. It was, moreover, my privilege to teach for eleven years (1963-74) at the School of Theology in Porto Novo which developed from the Seminary of which he speaks and is now able to award first degrees in Theology.

It seems that, though this is not an academic book, Parrinder possesses an invaluable source – a journal which he kept more assiduously than I did during my time in Africa. As a result, he is able to share with us, in vivid detail, events and impressions from his life as a young missionary. Some of his experiences, amusing in retrospect, were alarming at the time, and all are instructive.

In the 1930s and 1940s, life in West Africa was more basic, slower and in some ways more complicated than in the sixties and seventies. Water, for example, had to be drawn and carried in the Seminary as almost everywhere else. In later years, however, we had the pleasure of running water, electricity, bottled gas for cooking and the telephone. Later, too, there was no need to take a boat to reach Lagos, since a main road ran through Porto Novo to the frontier with Nigeria and on to that great city. Today the Marina in Lagos is a crowded one-way thoroughfare and an international road bypasses Porto Novo. Moreover, Porto Novo and the town of Cotonou are four times the size they were in 1974; and there is no more red dust on the road to Dassa Zoumé which is tarred right through, while Dassa itself has electricity and boasts a good small hotel-restaurant.

In other ways, too, the story can be updated. Harry Henry (p. 112), one of Parrinder's brilliant young students, has gone to his reward, after holding the presidency of the autonomous Methodist Church of Bénin (formerly

Dahomey) and exercising, in retirement, a remarkable ministry of reconciliation in Gabon. The son of Paul Hountodji (pp. 47-48, 50, 95, 99, 110) is a professor of Philosophy, and his story is typical of many. The church at Ouézoumé (p. 51ff.) was replaced by a larger, more substantial building, and at the centenary celebrations, which I was delighted to attend, the Rev Philip Potter (of Dominica and the World Council of Churches) preached.

Some things, however, do not change a great deal. Traditional religion and Islam remain strong influences, and the Institute of Theology, though augmented by the construction of a lay training and conference centre, retains its outward appearance. Catechists, on the other hand, are now trained in Togo, in collaboration with the church there, and Togolese students come to Porto Novo for their theological studies. The need to show that the Church is not a 'foreign body', however, is as great as ever. In 1992, therefore, the Methodist Church celebrated, with great ceremony in the outer courtyard of the palace at Abomey and the placing of a commemorative plaque, the 150th anniversary of the visit of Thomas Birch Freeman and his interview with King Guezo of Abomey.

In some circles, the fact that the Methodist Church, with its roots in Great Britain, exists in French-speaking countries of West Africa is often greeted with a mixture of surprise and curiosity. The curiosity can only be satisfied by three different historical explanations relating to the three countries involved – Bénin, Togo and Côte d'Ivoire; and the surprise may well be increased by the news that the Methodist Church in Bénin (at that time, Dahomey) existed as part of the Methodist District based in Lagos, Nigeria, before and after Dahomey became a French colony.

This complex background explains, in part, some of the difficulties experienced by Geoffrey and Mary Parrinder and their colleagues and vividly recounted in this book. Alongside the grind of everyday life, for example, we are given a taste of the tensions faced by a British-linked church existing under the Vichy regime in World War II. That this church was able to survive and grow, and in later years face other strenuous tests, is a cause of great thanksgiving. The reasons for such survival and growth may be complex, but the reaction of the old lady listening to Parrinder's exposition of one of Christ's parables (p. 128) seems crucial: 'I always knew there was something like that. I've been waiting for it all my life.'

The Gospel finds an echoing chord in people's lives, and that is the Church's strength.

This book, then, offers a series of fascinating glimpses of life from the point of view of a 'mission partner' (as we now say) in a particular place and a particular period. It helps us to put present developments in historical perspective and reminds us that Methodism is not involved only in the English-speaking parts of Africa. In this way, it may help to break the 'stranglehold' of Anglocentricity, where it still exists, in our thinking about the World Church. If, alongside this book, we could have a similar series of cameos of the same area and the same period written by an equally sensitive and percipient African writer, 'The Belly of the Snake' would be revealed as an even more interesting place!

As it is, we have a view, not otherwise easily obtainable, of life and labour at a crucial time in the life of the Methodist Church in Dahomey, and for that we can only be grateful.

Douglas Maw
Loughborough, September 2000

INTRODUCTION

In the *Journal of Religion in Africa* (October 1989) the editor, Adrian Hastings, wrote that 'for African history the 1940s are an understudied decade. The great public changes from the colonial era to the coming of Independence were still to come. The colonial order remained very much in place though it had manifestly run out of steam. The main Christian churches were now large, well established institutions, but with the world war they were unusually short of staff and hardly in an innovative mood. Even religious independency, whose vibrant growth is well documented for the twenties and thirties, appears relatively quiescent in these years.' Yet there were 'portents of a world to come', among them being 'the awakening concern with traditional religion of a young Methodist in Dahomey'.

This statement was alongside my article for Professor Hastings on 'Dahomey half a century ago'. Now, in the present book, I have tried to sketch something of the life and state of affairs in two decades, the 1930s and '40s, in the south-eastern and central parts of the former French colony of Dahomey.

This account begins with a description of travel from England, in a manner which has now completely changed. French and other continental mission workers for Dahomey usually went on French shipping lines from Bordeaux or Marseilles to the chief port of Cotonou, some twenty miles from inland Porto Novo. British staff most commonly sailed from Liverpool to Lagos and then by launch along the lagoon to Porto Novo, as will be described. Although we did sometimes travel through France, the customary Liverpool-Lagos route for the British was perhaps a hangover from the days when Methodist work in Dahomey was ruled from Nigeria, forming part of its Yoruba Mission. From the headquarters in Lagos missionaries were sent up country in Nigeria and westwards to Dahomey. The system worked well enough, apart from an uncomfortable lagoon journey, until the European war broke off relations between France and Britain and their colonies, with unhappy consequences, as will be seen.

Why go to a French colony? That was almost accidental. In the thirties there was a struggling church and mission in Porto Novo and neighbourhood. Obliged by the government to conduct all religious and educational work in French, the church was forced to recruit workers from any place or country that could help. In 1932 an urgent appeal came to Richmond College in the University of London, where I was studying theology. As I had done well in school French, and was interested in Africa, I offered my services. Then I was advised by a French fellow-student to become more proficient in spoken French, and I was offered a year's bursary at the University of Montpellier. After this experience I was sent to seminary teaching in Dahomey and the Ivory Coast, and later went to the University College of Ibadan in Nigeria. Of eight years in Dahomey six were spent in Porto Novo in teaching, but there was plenty of time for travel, and my research into African religion began there.

My lifelong interest has been in religion, in its broadest sense. After a Christian upbringing and training, it was Buddhism that first attracted my attention through a friend, and then Islam in northern Africa. My understanding of 'African Traditional Religion' (a term that I may claim to have invented, and that others have used) was partly shaped by study of the historical and literary religions. It seemed important to consider African religion in the manner of the study of world religions, and there were many parallels, for example with the gods and customs of ancient Egypt or Greece, or with modern Hinduism. There are problems with this approach but also advantages, in that African religion is not taken as isolated from the rest of the world or scorned as mere fetishism or superstition, but as having its own traditions and history, even where unwritten, and with its social and personal characteristics.

I had particular assignments in Africa, mostly in teaching, administration or research. Later as a university teacher in Africa, and again in England, I was formally 'permitted to labour with an external organization', in the curious jargon of the Methodist Church at that time. I was still under the overseas missionary department, though I must say that its control was exercised lightly, after one or two clarifications.

When I became involved in the study and description of African indigenous religion, and later with aspects of Asian religions, and wrote much on them, some friends did not know that formally I was a missionary and were surprised if they found out. It might be questioned or implied that a Christian worker, even in an 'external organization', was a propagandist, who could hardly be fair to other religions since he was bound to think them mistaken and seek to convert their followers.

5

It must be stated plainly that I tried not to see things through 'mission spectacles', or with any sense of disapproval. Everybody has his or her point of view, even with 'anthropological spectacles' or 'atheistic spectacles', but most scholars try consciously to see practices in context and describe them impartially. They do not judge, but give accounts of things as they are, usually with sympathy.

It may also be said that the fair and detached viewpoint was taken over from training. At Richmond, though a theological college, there were lectures and studies on Islam, Zoroastrianism, Hinduism and Buddhism. These were formal, providing information on history and teachings, and the tutor might have no specialist knowledge of these faiths. But there was no propaganda or apologetic, and we were never told that these religions were mistaken in doctrines or practices. Having Buddhist friends, I would have been sensitive to criticism of their beliefs. Occasionally, experts and believers in the religions themselves were invited to speak to the students, and to receive and answer questions.

1. TO THE WHITE MAN'S GRAVE

Every Wednesday in the 1930s a passenger mail ship of Elder Dempster Lines left Liverpool for various ports in British-ruled West Africa. In the afternoon of 6th September 1933, having come from London by the train which ran on to Liverpool docks, I boarded the m.v.*Adda* for the twelve-day journey to Lagos in Nigeria.

The *Adda* was one of four regular passenger ships in the service and, with its list to port, was regarded as an old tub. From 1951 a newer and bigger boat, the *Aureol*, was much superior, as we found when we finally left Nigeria on it in 1958. It had its own swimming pool, whereas on the *Adda* only a large canvas bath was put up on deck for passengers to splash about in when we reached tropical waters.

I had been booked into Second Class and went down two decks to inspect what documents had termed my 'stateroom'. This cabin was L-shaped, with two bunks on one side and another in the foot of the L, and a short passage led to a closed porthole, which provided the only natural light. There was no running water, and every morning the English steward filled a small tank over a basin to give washing water. He would bring hot water in cans for shaving, on request, and there were public bathrooms along the corridor. There was no air-conditioning in the cabins and they became hot in the tropics.

I was given the top bunk and two miners the other beds. I hardly saw them for the whole journey, for they slept late, spent all day in the bar and came back after midnight.

In those days there was no regular service to West Africa, but when several lines started after the Second World War, with BOAC, Air France, and national lines later, most travellers preferred the quicker air services and only used ships for heavy baggage. Finally, the *Aureol* was the last passenger mail ship to sail from Liverpool in 1972, and Elder Dempster Lines were sold off in 1989.

Deck space on the *Adda* was restricted, with a warning notice put on a railing each morning: 'Second Class Passengers Not Allowed Beyond This Point'. A similar notice shut off the smaller Third Class quarters and up to

200 deck passengers who were taken along the tropical regions off the West African coast from Freetown to Lagos.

In front of us were much longer decks where the First Class played games, but we could all march around the ship for exercise every morning before breakfast. After that, mingling of classes was only permitted for a few purposes, such as Sunday worship, which was open to all passengers in the First Class lounge.

Every Sunday morning there was an official religious service, using the Anglican *Book of Common Prayer* and *Hymns Ancient and Modern*. If there was a missionary in First or Second Class, the purser presented the captain's compliments and requested professional aid. If there was no help available, the captain himself might rattle through the morning liturgy of the Prayer Book, with hymns like 'O God, our help in ages past' or 'Eternal Father, strong to save'. The services were usually well attended, chiefly by missionaries and administrators and their wives.

I soon found friends of various churches in Second Class, though bishops travelled First. I met an independent missionary from Third Class and debated his fundamentalist view of all Africa under the rule of the devil. Other missionaries were going to established churches in Gambia, Sierra Leone, Gold Coast and Nigeria, and I was bound for Dahomey in French West Africa. We made up a bridge party, not playing for money, and joined in excursions ashore at stops. I had only seven pounds in my wallet and could not have spent much at the bar even if I had wanted to. Coffee was served on deck by stewards in mid-morning, and ice-creams in the tropics, and tea was available in the dining-room in the afternoon.

The Second Class dining-room was pleasant and roomy, and the food good and plentiful, though traditional and generally unimaginative. If we worked through the breakfast and lunch menus, that was almost enough, and lack of much exercise for twelve days soon reduced appetites. Portions of food were sometimes small and a friend at my table told the steward, 'If that's an 'omelette', bring me an 'omme'.'

Most passengers were white and British, as were the waiters and cabin stewards. Coloured stewards began to appear later, when the service was being run down. There were some African passengers, who were placed at their own tables in the dining-room, and there was little mixing. Only later did racial discrimination weaken, and we travelled home in 1958, from the University College of Ibadan in Nigeria, with my colleague the Igbo historian Kenneth Diké and his family, in First Class, sitting together at meals and on deck. Even then, Kenneth made the first move, saying that he did not want to be placed by the stewards among unknown coloured people.

There were no children on our journey on the *Adda* in 1933, though there were plenty of women among the 330 passengers. The British believed white children could not survive on the West Coast of Africa, which they still thought of as the White Man's Grave. They derided the French who took children to their African colonies: 'The French, you know . . . Their children are pasty little kids with sores on their legs. They keep them in cages of mosquito-proof netting, like monkeys, and if they are let out, they wear huge sun helmets. It isn't fair to them.'

Hardbitten Old Coasters declared that Africa was not for white women. Most of them had never heard of Mary Slessor or Mary Kingsley in West Africa 50 years earlier. But the strains on women who had left children at home were at times almost visible.

The great change came again after the Second World War, with less inhibited university and other professional people taking families with them. By then there were better health conditions, and yellow fever, the chief enemy, had been conquered. In the fifties most ships provided crèches, employed nurses, and had swimming pools. The children ran all over the ship, leant over the side and enjoyed sun and sea.

All Europeans wore sun helmets in the 1930s, as did many Africans, and helmets appeared like spring blossoms when we entered the tropics. Topees were white or khaki, round or oblong, with green or red lining. Some ladies wore double felt hats. I had taken a short medical course at Livingstone College in east London and a doctor, 'with long experience of Africa', had warned us that 'the graveyards along the Coast are full of the bodies of fools who went out in the sun without hats'. Topees must be worn from sunrise to sunset, and even the garden should not be crossed without a hat. That there was often more cloud and humidity than direct sun's heat in West Africa was explained by saying that the 'deadly miasma' magnified the sun's rays and made them more dangerous than in clearer and hotter regions in the north.

During the Second World War, however, after the North Africa landings in 1942, armies of Allied soldiers came from Senegal and Sierra Leone along West Africa, making new routes to the east, towards the Sudan and Egypt, which broke through colonial boundaries. International roads were built and camps erected at many points. The soldiers were issued with felt hats, but most threw them off and worked in the sun stripped to the waist. The Old Coasters sat back and waited complacently for the 'inevitable' death toll. It did not come, and at last the penny dropped: hats were not necessary. Sun helmets were therefore put away, and in the universities later they were almost unknown. I wore a topee for my first ten years in West Africa, and no hat at all for the second ten years. Only some Africans continued to wear sun helmets, and some French people who went to the hot and dry Sahara regions. Sunglasses, however, remained as useful protection from the glare, especially for those with light-coloured eyes.

Livingstone in central Africa and Baikie on the Niger in the 1850s had taken quinine as protection against malarial fever, because Jesuits in South America had learnt its value from the Indians. But the causes of malaria were unknown until Manson in 1894 identified it as coming not from 'bad air', as 'malaria' suggested, but from mosquito bites. In 1933, therefore, we all took quinine, one large white tablet a day, from the moment the ship drew into an African port at Freetown, since the insects might fly into the ship when it docked. Later we had various refinements of medication, Paludrine and others, and we talked of the world conquest of malaria, which has not happened.

Our baggage was in metal trunks, to protect the contents from being eaten by white ants, or in wooden crates if we risked them. We had been issued with Outfit Lists and generous grants for tropical kit. There were special outfitters in London and Liverpool. By the thirties tents and sunshades no longer figured on the lists. I never needed a tent, but slept in many African huts on my camp-bed. But we could get collapsible washing bowls and baths, and – what was especially important – water filters. Tropical suits were indicated, white and khaki, in cotton, with detachable buttons for easy washing. There were shirts and shorts, Aertex underwear, long white or khaki cotton stockings, and boots or sandals. 'Mosquito boots' had long loose leather uppers which slipped under trousers in the evenings and protected ankles from mosquito bites. These were useful and comfortable, and some ladies had longer boots which covered their knees but could get very hot.

One item on the list was a 'cholera belt'. There was little or no cholera in West Africa, but this sort of corset was meant to be put on under pyjamas at night to guard against the chill breeze that might blow in the middle of the night and cause 'coast tummy'. A length of flannel to be wrapped round the body provided a simpler version. Both objects were soon found to bring on a common and painful rash on the skin, known as 'prickly heat'. Since we came to sleep naked in the tropics, it was easy to keep a bit of sheet round the waist in case that much needed night breeze did come.

Other items were suggestions of foods to take: tinned milk, butter and necessities or luxuries which might be available in shops in big towns but not in country places. Some people stocked up enough for their 18-month tour and lived on tinned foods nearly every day. Others were limited by the money available or learnt to live on the produce of the country.

We had been out of sight of land in the Atlantic since Wednesday, and the green hills of the isle of Madeira appeared with the new week, to great rejoicing. The *Adda* pulled into harbour and stayed all day, and most passengers rushed ashore. Several of us shared a car to go into the mountains, and then visited some of the town shops. Once we looked into a casino, and watched the jaded players. The docks were lined with salesmen and women with all manner of embroidered cloths and basket work, and they soon swarmed up on the ship. On the other side little canoes appeared with brown lads calling out to the remaining passengers, 'Small boy, I dive.' They plunged into the sea as people threw down coins.

Elder Dempster ships called on alternate weeks at Portuguese Madeira, or at Las Palmas or Tenerife in the Spanish Canary Isles. At Las Palmas in 1936 we saw crowds of conscript soldiers in rough green or khaki uniforms being drilled for despatch to Franco's fascist army in the Spanish Civil War. One of our party supported Franco, as defender of the Church, but most were for the legitimate republican government of Spain, and there were disputes about that bitter conflict.

The first sight of Africa came as we lay out to sea off Bathurst (now Banjul) in Gambia, and the low flat line of land in the hazy distance looked unattractive. Sierra Leone was better, with its 'lion hills', green and lush. We went into Freetown harbour and took a car up to Fourah Bay College, on a splendid hill site. At that time it was the nearest British West African colonies came to producing higher education, through links with Durham

11

University. Some days later we lay out to sea off Accra in the Gold Coast (Ghana). Although it was the capital of the country, there was no proper harbour. Bulky goods were unloaded by crane into large canoes manned by oarsmen, and into them also nervous passengers for Accra were lowered in 'mammy chairs', wooden boxes with seats. It looked risky, and the swell of the sea often made it hard for cranemen to direct people and goods into boats. As we watched, one of the heavy loads slipped into the sea, to be rescued with frantic struggles. The black navvies were stripped to the waist, their muscular bodies gleaming in the sun.

'Look like apes, don't they?' remarked a man at my side. It was one of my cabin miners who had come out from the bar. A stream of sewage was flushed from one of the ship's bathrooms, as plumbers worked to remove a blockage. It showered into a canoe and the labourers shook their fists and swore back in fury.

'Why don't you try to convert them?' he continued. 'They're so intellectual.'

'I suppose our stevedores at home can look dirty and ugly,' I replied, facing the first challenge in defence of missions. 'How would they react to such provocation? The air would be even bluer. They need a bath first.'

Then from the shore came a canoe paddled by a large negro, wearing only a loin cloth under a battered top hat, and a clerical collar. He chanted in a mocking voice, to a revivalist tune:

> Hallelujah, I'm a bum bum,
> Hallelujah, bum again,
> Hallelujah, here I come now,
> To invite you again.

'Big boy, I dive!' he shouted. He refused to dive in the sea for coppers, but plunged overboard when somebody threw down a silvery coin. If he bit it and found it was French money, he shook his head and let out a stream of curses.

'A bright product of the missions,' said my neighbour.

'There are frauds in every country,' was all I could think of answering.

12

When the *Adda* finally arrived at Lagos in Nigeria and docked in the harbour, the wharf was full of soldiers and government officials, while a military band played a tattoo. In Second Class we had hardly realised that the Governor of Nigeria, Sir Bernard Bourdillon, was a traveller on our ship, and he had to land before the rest of us could go ashore. After a long wait, he descended the gangway in white suit and plumed sun helmet to be greeted by his court, of white officials first and then African chiefs and lesser beings.

The Governor was followed after an interval by the King of Benin, the Oba of Nigerian Benin, and his wives, who were received with enthusiasm by a large crowd from the rear. They came forward and prostrated themselves on the concrete wharf before their traditional ruler. It was rumoured that the Oba had complained that during his visit to England he had only been received at the British Empire Office, and had not met his fellow King of England.

We landed late in the afternoon and our small party was welcomed and taken by car to the Methodist Boys' High School on Lagos Marina.

* * * * *

There is no need to recount all my sea journeys to West Africa, but two other highlights may be mentioned here.

In 1936 I travelled home from Port Bouet in the Ivory Coast on board a small German banana cargo boat, the *Wahehe*, which went at speed with its precious contents. There were only a dozen passengers, all in one class, and accommodation, food and service were good. There were piles of Nazi propaganda papers and leaflets in the lounge, though nobody seemed to look at them. But at dinner each evening the menus were printed with pictures of former German colonies: Togo, Kamerun, Tanganyika, Rwanda, South-west Africa. Then for its English passengers the *Wahehe* called at Southampton; and, as we sailed up the Solent, a band of the ship's staff played music on the bridge, while German passengers and officers brought out binoculars to study the fortifications, such as they were.

In the autumn of 1943 the Second World War was still raging, but the submarine menace was almost conquered and I returned to Africa from Liverpool in a large convoy. Off Belfast and Glasgow we picked up other ships and then went far out into the Atlantic and did not see land again till Freetown two weeks later. It was a huge armada of ships of many nations, with naval corvettes and frigates, and a destroyer guarding the outside limits and checking that no lights showed at night. We heard later that the previous week a German aeroplane had come out from occupied France and had sunk three ships in a similar British convoy, and while passengers had mostly been picked up from the sea, they were crowded on the decks of naval vessels till they could be landed in Allied-occupied North Africa.

A convoy sails at the speed of the slowest ship and we went along gently at about five knots. Elder Dempster's fleet had been commandeered for war work, and a New Zealand boat, hired to help West African trade, had been built for colder waters and became very hot once tropical regions were entered, and some of us took bedding to sleep on deck. But there were some prize Scotch bulls being carried to Argentina. The poor beasts, though given blocks of ice to lick and cooled by fans, felt the growing heat in the open hold, and one by one they collapsed. Every other morning, it seemed, a huge bull carcase was thrown overboard, yet we human beings could survive. Less than half the bulls were left when we reached Freetown, and then the ship sped on to Argentina by itself in the safer waters of the south Atlantic. We were landed in Sierra Leone and, after a week spent in a transit camp, were put on a smaller ship, from Labrador this time, for a fast and uneventful trip along the coast to Lagos.

2. UNDER THE SWASTIKA

The Methodist Boys' High School in Lagos had a fine position on the Marina, facing the lagoon and the sea beyond. In front of the school compound, a road, not too busy in those days, was fringed by a grassy bank on which occasional fishermen waited patiently by the swirling brown waters of the lagoon. There was great excitement once when we saw a shark dragged ashore and immediately cut up.

The school grounds held classrooms and, as a main feature by the road, a large two-storey house in South African style, which had living rooms above and school and mission offices on the ground floor. When passing through Lagos, I stayed mostly with the Jacksons, the headmaster and his wife. They were very hospitable and later, during the war, opened their house on many evenings to visiting soldiers.

'There is a launch to Porto Novo this afternoon,' said Bill Mann, the mission secretary, on the morning after my arrival. 'I can run you down in the car to the Woermann office for your ticket later.'

'I can go now if it isn't too far,' I replied. 'I would prefer to walk to get to the feel of the place.'

'Suit yourself. It will get hotter. I'll send a boy with you as guide. Do you want some money?'

'I have hardly any left.'

'I can give you enough for yourself and the ticket, and debit the account of Dahomey.'

It seemed cool as I set off with a schoolboy, and a light morning breeze was deceptively fresh. Soon sweat began to run down our faces and chests, and patches appeared under the arms of khaki shirts. The road back to the docks was lined with coconut palm trees, and numbers of people increased as we came to low-lying shops and offices and some larger buildings. There were no skyscrapers yet, but we passed a tall Anglican cathedral and a storeyed post office. The crowds grew as we neared the shipping area, people pushing and slipping in front of us. When I stepped over a deep drain into the road, with its hooting cars and overloaded lorries, people shouted in protest and a driver called out, 'Hey, Mister Man. Make you walk on path.'

We struggled through the crowds: a man singing out as he wheeled a hand cart beside the deep gutter, a woman in a blue gown carrying a huge bunch of green bananas on her head, boys running round our ankles. It was hard for a new arrival to distinguish features in the shiny black faces, and only slowly did recognition of differences develop.

The palm trees came to an end, giving way to black huts of the dock offices and concrete hangars. The *Adda* had been towed over to the Apapa wharves opposite and another liner towered beside the quay. Beyond this complex, on the right-hand side of the road, was a whitewashed building of the Woermann shipping line of Hamburg. It faced a bay of the lagoon and a wharf where small boats were clustered.

'Here is the office for your ticket to Dahomey,' said my guide. 'I will leave you as I want to go to the market. I expect you can find your way back to the school. Just follow the road we came on.'

I turned into the Woermann building, between two white concrete posts. An African doorkeeper in khaki shirt and shorts, with red fez and bare feet, saluted me and pointed to a steep flight of stairs. In the office above a fair-haired young German clerk clicked his heels, inspected passport and papers, and went into a back room to get a ticket.

'My God, that fellow's here already,' said a low growl.

I turned and saw a red-faced man, of medium height, standing by the window. He wore a white open-necked shirt, white shorts and stockings, and shiny brown leather shoes. He pointed to a picture on the wall, a photograph of Adolf Hitler. It was 1933 and the Nazis had just come to power in Germany.

'Is it prudence, or do they like that joker?' he asked. 'Are you going to Dahomey as well?'

I agreed, and he continued, 'Are you French?'

16

'No, but I've just come from France.'

'That's useful, for I'm told French is essential in Dahomey. I shall have a struggle. I got my move because in a weak moment I admitted to school French, long ago.'

After more than sixty years I have forgotten his name. Was it John Adams? But his presence and general conversation remain clear in my mind. He talked easily and got on with most people, white and black. In his early thirties, he was regarded as middle-aged on the West African coast, but he was active and imaginative, and his drive in business and social relations gained him steady promotion. His appointment to his firm's ancient shop and store in French Dahomey might have been regarded by others as a trial, or even a relegation, but the place needed modernising or closing, and Adams had accepted the challenge. He nodded at the picture again.

'He doesn't like blacks.'

'Keep them in their place. Paternalism, like Leopold in the Congo.'

'He's a threat to peace, too.'

'Germany is only asking for the return of her colonies, which Britain and France took away after the war.'

'Only! These boys are aggressive. Why do you think they have offices in most of the countries round Africa? Look out of the window. We shall be under the swastika this afternoon. Our launch is flying the crooked cross. I must be quiet, here comes the young brown shirt.'

The blond clerk returned, gave us tickets from Nigeria to Dahomey and wished us a safe journey. Half expecting a Nazi salute, we turned our backs quickly and went down the stairs.

'Haven't you got a car?' asked Adams. 'My driver's over there. I can drop you wherever you want and pick you up again for the launch at two o'clock.'

'No, thank you. I prefer to walk, and I want to look in the shops.'

'Just as you like. See you at two.'

Lagos was the capital of Nigeria, and Nigeria was under British rule, while Dahomey to the west was a French colony. Despite being neighbours in rival empires for over forty years, or perhaps because of the rivalry, the two countries were not connected, in the thirties, by any road or rail services or any passenger air flights. Travellers wanting to go from one colony to the other, as we did, had either to take a motor launch along the lagoon from Lagos to Porto Novo, or struggle miles up country through swamps and by forest paths. When we tried this bush route with a car years later, it was very tricky and depended on the rains holding off.

By irony, or political and military scheming, the launch service ('la pétrolette', as the French called it) between British and French territories was organised by a German shipping company. It probably did not pay, but whether it showed commercial enterprise by the Woermann Line or was meant to serve as a base for the recovery of old German colonies in Togo to the west and the Cameroons in the east, nothing was said openly. We did not discover whether the German clerks put the picture of Hitler up from prudence or because they supported him. Probably the latter, and they may have been agents preparing to take back the old German colonies from the British and French. When war broke out in 1939 the Woermann Line offices were closed and any German staff who had stayed were interned.

We travellers to Dahomey left Lagos in early afternoon, with a swastika flag hanging limply at the stern of the boat. The young German clerk saw us off efficiently and with no sign of Nazi influence, and the Nigerian captain of the launch welcomed us and tried to make us comfortable.

The launch was really a motor barge, with a covered hold in the middle full of goods for export. Adams and I were the only white passengers and were offered a tiny hot cabin. After a brief look, however, we chose to remain in the open and deck-chairs were placed for us under an awning over the tarpaulin on planks that covered the hold. A score or more African passengers sprawled along narrow gangways and in a clearing at the back, with bundles of clothes, food, bunches of bananas, large plantains, sacks of yams, baskets of chickens and tethered goats. There was noise, shouts and laughter. Young girls were stripped to the waist, in the country custom of those days, and mothers untied babies off their backs and suckled them.

The lagoon was neither blue nor coral-bound, as might have been imagined. It was a muddy expanse of water that stretched from the Lagos wharves to a distant sandbar with trees. Part of it swirled towards the open sea where liners came in, but our launch soon swung westwards along narrowing creeks in the glare of the sinking sun.

Before long on the banks of both sides of the lagoon, or sluggish river, there appeared mangrove swamps and occasional plantations of tall and graceful coconut palms. From time to time a brightly coloured bird flashed through the branches of the mangroves which trailed in the murky waters. Then it was gone, and everything seemed still. There were plops of fish in the water, but nothing else to reveal the life that must have teemed below the surface of the fertile tropical stream. The sun beat down implacably, and was reflected from the lagoon, the hot and humid air only being tempered by the steady movement of the boat.

The launch drew in to a jetty, at a clearing on the right bank where palm trees surrounded a group of thatched mud huts, and it seemed that the whole population crowded down to greet the weekly barge. Some women landed with their babies and bundles of goods they had bought in the town. Passengers were taken aboard and, in a few minutes, the launch was off again.

'I've been moved from John Holt's in Calabar to their store in Porto Novo,' remarked Adams, as we sat side by side under the awning. 'What did you say your firm was?'

'I didn't,' I answered. 'It's the Protestant mission in Dahomey, linked to our work in Lagos.'

'I noticed you came to the wharf in a car with Methodist Boys' High School on the side. And you look like a missionary.'

'What look is that?'

'A serious air, and you haven't much baggage. No crates of whisky, unless they're stored somewhere else.'

'There are suitcases and boxes of books,' I said. 'But it's true that I think missionaries should be temperate, if not teetotal, and I imagine most of them are.'

'Except the Catholic priests,' replied Adams. 'They can be boon companions. But even they are an odd lot, like yours.'

'What do you mean?'

'Why did you come on this caper?'

'To serve the country,' I replied.

'Which you had never seen. Very high-minded. Good intentions but, I fancy, a little understatement. Don't you really mean to save souls, snatch them from the gaping grave?'

'That's how it used to be put.'

'Assuming they've got souls. They've certainly got bodies. Aren't the girls attractive? Are you married?'

'No. Not yet.'

'Then it's an engagement ring you're wearing on your left hand. You're not a monk. But you'll have problems. They all do, like the rest of us. Probably all mad, to come to places like this.'

'Are you mad also?' I asked. 'Traders and government officials?'

'We're here for the money,' he answered bluntly. 'Much more than we could get in England. But we're a mixture too. Philanthropists or mad, most of us, and perhaps there isn't much difference.'

The boat pulled in at another village pier, and a few people crowded down a bank to wave. Naked boys and girls swam alongside in the muddy water, splashing and calling. Some people got off and others joined our launch.

Adams had a paper on his lap, but as we left the village he spoke again.

'Tell me, we're strangers, but thrown together and I'm curious. Why are you, an Englishman, going to a mission in a French colony?'

'It is an old British foundation,' I replied. 'But the work is in French, as their colonial government has insisted it must be. They were short of French-speaking Protestant workers, and I had qualified in the language and was interested in Africa.'

'I see that. But why is your English mission still on the French side? Are you spying, like the German shipping company?

'Not at all. It's for the same reason, I believe, as your shops and stores are there. Our Church, which is in many countries, was established in what are now Nigeria and Dahomey long before the British and French colonial armies in the 1890s drew the straight dividing lines between their new conquests on maps which they thought were blank.'

'I wonder if we shall stick it out much longer under the Frogs?' queried Adams. 'John Holt's seemed undecided whether to expand or give in to a French trading company. But there's a lot of good palm oil about.'

'We shall stay,' I declared. 'We were there before the French or the British came, and we shall be there when they have gone.'

'Even if they get independence, or turn to Communism?'

'It was a French reformer', I assured him, 'who told the King of France: "The church, sire, is an anvil which has broken many hammers"!'

'Bully for him,' said Adams, and he turned again to leaf through a weekly edition of the *Daily Mirror*.

In the early evening the launch drew in at the sizeable town of Badagry, an old slaving outpost now in decline and separated from the sea by a wide sandbar. This was the last stop in Nigeria and it grew dark as we left and forged along the lagoon westwards.

'The Jerries assured me we should be at Porto Novo before night,' exclaimed Adams after a time. 'We could just make it. The hulks are ahead . . . Damn those smooth liars, we're dropping anchor.'

21

Through the dusk we saw yellow lights and could just trace the outlines of two large boats moored in midstream. These so-called 'hulks' replaced the trading stations of the former slaving ruffians and palm oil coasters. In the 1930s they were two-storey houseboats which served, at the nominal frontier, as living quarters for the police and customs officers of each of the adjoining colonies. There was no sign of life on the Nigerian hulk and the captain of our launch made profuse apologies to his exasperated passengers, but insisted that he dared not venture past in the dark for fear that he might lose his licence and we might be shot at from one of the hulks.

'Now we shall be bitten to pieces by mosquitoes,' complained Adams. 'We can't get off, and I bet you haven't got a net with you. But I've brought this brandy. Have some, it's the only protection. If, in the swamps of the Niger delta, I drained a bottle, I was too sloshed to feel the bites in the first half of the night, and in the second half the midges were too drunk to bite. You're not a fanatical teetotaller, are you?'

'They had wine at my theological college in Montpellier,' I said. 'But I have never tried spirits, though they might be useful for medicinal purposes.'

'Then let me be your doctor for the night. Drink this. Now wrap a newspaper round your ankles and any other tender spots. Bits of the *Daily Mirror* will do fine. These are vicious insects. They've bitten through the canvas of the chairs already, but I doubt if their teeth will get through the paper. We shall have to sweat the night out.'

Passengers and crew tried to settle down in the dark, covering themselves with cloths and sheets, while mosquitoes buzzed around, biting everybody. It was hot under the papers and clothes but, if they were thrown off to get some air, the insects came like armies. Then towards morning it got a little cooler and people shivered and coughed. Adams and I stirred at first light and breakfasted on brandy and biscuits.

It was another hour before there was any movement on the Nigerian hulk, and then unshaven African clerks beckoned the launch to the side and stamped the ship's papers. As we drew away, a European appeared on the upper deck of the hulk, bearded, tousled and in crumpled pyjamas. He stared at the launch with an air of seeming despair at being marooned in the mosquito-ridden lagoon.

22

On the Dahomean side, two clerks came on board the barge, demanding passports and identity cards, scanning and stamping them. Having made a superficial examination of the baggage and peered into the hold, they waved the boat on. Cigarette ends hung from their mouths and ash spilled down their shabby uniforms. Everything about them underlined their isolation from the rest of their own country. And they ignored the other hulk.

In the glare of morning the launch finally drew alongside a wharf at Porto Novo, the capital town of Dahomey. There was a line of quays and more activity than in the villages. But the humid heat made sweat run off the bodies of the alighting travellers.

3. DAHOMEY-BÉNIN

From the sixteenth century onwards there had been great interest for Europeans in some of the ancient kingdoms of West Africa. One of the most notorious places was Dahomey, which I had now reached, and travellers wrote of visits to its capital town Abomey. The name Dahomey was derived from the snake, the python, which was called Dan, and the country was Dan-homé, 'Dan's belly', a land under the patronage of the sacred and untouchable python.

There were temples for the python divinity in many places, especially along rivers and by the sea. A famous snake-temple was, and still is, to be seen at Ouidah (Whydah) on the Dahomean coast, but there were others at Abomey, Porto Novo and elsewhere, so that even beyond the notorious kingdom one was still within 'the belly of the snake'.

The capitals of some of these African kingdoms were often called 'cities of blood', from ancient 'customs' in which human lives had been sacrificed, and in the same countries prisoners from local wars were supplied to European slave traders bound for the Americas.

In the 1890s both 'customs' and slavery were ended by international actions, and the scramble for African empires was undertaken by British, French, German, Spanish and Portuguese. Dahomey was conquered by French armies in 1894 and became part of their imperial French West Africa (Afrique Occidentale Française), between German Togoland and British-ruled Nigeria.

The French colony of Dahomey was a long thin stretch of country, including previously separate territories far beyond the ancient kingdom of Dahomey, from the coastline to the river Niger in the north. Moreover, for French administration the capital town of the new colony of Dahomey was fixed near the coast at Porto Novo, which though ancient had never belonged to the old Dahomey. It was a centre of the Goun-Yoruba peoples and near the frontier of Yoruba-dominated western Nigeria.

While cities of blood and colonial empires held their sway, Christian missions of different kinds were active at many places along the West

African coast, though not far into the interior. In Dahomey, however, of Protestants only the Wesleyan Methodist Church from Britain was at work, chiefly in the area round Porto Novo where it had arrived in 1862. In due time, it was the sole Protestant Church that was given official recognition by the new French rulers in their colony of Dahomey.

I lived in Porto Novo from 1933, with intervals at other places, and references to the life and history of Dahomey are in the following pages and in parts of other books. In my records Dahomey refers chiefly to Porto Novo and the northern region of Dassa Zoumé. I did indeed visit the ancient centre of Abomey, and met the descendant of former kings, but Dahomey in this book indicates especially Porto Novo and Dassa.

Now the very name of Dahomey has vanished from the map, being officially replaced by the title Bénin since 1975. This change originated with local governments largely composed of people from the coastal areas who had repudiated suggestions that they were connected with the old slaving realm of Dahomey. Yet the name Bénin which they adopted is confusing and hardly appropriate, since an ancient city and kingdom of Bénin is hundreds of miles away to the east, in mid-Nigeria (we met the Oba of Benin coming off the ship in chapter one). If the country, and now the independent state, of Dahomey or Bénin is to survive, it should have a more suitable name. The confusion arises from the diversity of peoples and is a legacy of colonialism.

It is strange to think that over sixty-five years ago I lived in a country whose name has disappeared. Even in those days it was regarded from larger and richer Nigeria as poor, narrow, thinly populated and backward, not to mention French-ruled and with different official and local languages. Yet Dahomey, as it was in the broad sense, was full of interest, and part of the justification of my story is that it provides records of things and people that otherwise might have no memorial.

The religion of Dahomey, and neighbouring parts of West Africa, was described in my first book, *West African Religion,* published by the Epworth Press in 1949, and later enlarged and reprinted, with hardback and paperback editions, and a French translation. This has long been out of print and this present book seeks to provide more personal detail, put flesh on the bones, and show what life in Dahomey was like: for Africans and Europeans, ministers and catechists, college students and school children, priests and devotees, chiefs and administrators, in religious and secular activities.

We shall look at the religion of Dahomey in greater detail in chapter eight, but some brief comments at this point may be helpful. The word 'voodoo', known to the wider public from West Indian usage, had its origin in Dahomey where *vudu* or *vodoun* was and still is a common name for a god or spiritual being. Countless *vodouns* were revered in different regions of Dahomey; some of them I noted in *West African Religion* and others are mentioned below. The Voodoo of Haiti arose from a mixture of Dahomean and Christian religion, since most of the people there were descended from slaves imported from Dahomey and they had been evangelized by Roman Catholic priests.

In the region of Porto Novo, as in Abomey and other traditional towns, perhaps not at every street corner but at very many in the thirties, there were little wayside shrines. Generally, these were small thatched shelters covering clay mounds or simple wooden images, representing the guardian spirits of the place. Most of them have now disappeared from view, or are confined to quiet corners of compounds, and it may be difficult to envisage what old West African towns looked like. Here memory can help, for those of us who were present in the almost medieval settings.

The shrines, larger temples, 'convents', secret societies, local and public rituals, formed a complex of religion which has not completely disappeared but has undoubtedly shrunk or retreated from public view. Colonial and then nationalistic government, education, commerce, Christian missions, Islam and international contacts have all contributed to change the picture of place and society. It is important to obtain and preserve accounts of former times, so that the history may be recorded and perhaps some lessons learnt from it.

Amos Tutuola, the Nigerian novelist, when asked about the apparently haphazard series of his 'ghost towns', remarked simply, 'That is how I came to them.' Similarly the people, places and incidents in this book are how I came to them. Even the conversations given below, if not mechanically recorded in exactness, are how they have remained with me over the years. They represent life in Porto Novo and Dassa Zoumé 'as it came to me' in the thirties and forties of the last century. Interpretations themselves are recognized by historians as part of the events. There is no such thing as completely impartial history, and even science now acknowledges the role played by the scientist himself, with his own assumptions and interpretations.

The history is in the activity of people and the course of events. Looking back, many of the travels of Europeans to West Africa in the early years of the twentieth century, their dress, food and attitudes, seem to be strange and dated, yet it is important to record how they were. The presence of Germans between British and French colonies in the inter-war years, often ignored, surely deserves mention. The activities of Christian missions, justified or criticized, are part of the picture, with the emergence of self-governing African churches.

The struggles of a British Protestant mission with a French government involved minor incidents, misunderstandings, and, from some individuals and officials, suspicions of spying even in peacetime. These events and reactions were aggravated by the impossibility of return from leave when France and Britain had broken off diplomatic relations during wartime, and they culminated, as needs to be recorded and remembered, in the arrest of a young English missionary and his death in a French African prison.

This personal account ends long before the arrival of political independence for Dahomey in 1960 and the later trials of the Church under a short-lived Marxism. But that is another story, and it is to be hoped that those who passed through those years will write down their experiences.

4. INTO THE SNAKE'S BELLY

'The most mosquito-ridden town on the West Coast' was a common judgement on Porto Novo. The turbid lagoon in front of the town and stagnant swamps behind bred countless midges, which hung about by day and invaded all the houses and huts at night.

A collection of wharves along the lagoonside, metal, concrete and wooden, marked the property of trading companies, and behind them were some two or three-storey shops and offices. The launch had pulled in to one of the larger piers, which was crowded with people expecting relatives and friends, and at the back of the crowd I saw two figures waving at me. I said goodbye to Adams, who was met by a colleague, and turned to meet John Watson and his wife who had come to welcome the launch.

'Did you have a good journey?' asked John.

'Well . . .'

'Yes, I know, it is always the same if the launch leaves in the afternoon and has to spend all night on the lagoon. They should keep to a morning service.'

The Watsons were newly married, and although he had been in Porto Novo before, they both looked frail and were soon to be invalided home for good. John was tall and thin, dark-haired and dressed in spotless white suit and sun helmet. Jackie Watson had auburn hair and freckles, and her fair skin showed up mosquito bites which merged to bring intense irritation. She had been warned to bring out mosquito boots and had a long brown suede pair which came above her knees, tied by laces at the top and covered by her light dress. She seemed to be singled out by the insects and, to protect legs and knees, took to wearing the heavy boots all day, only to find that they made her hot and produced rashes. She had a wide sun helmet with red lining, which reflected on her face and made her look hotter still. Jackie never seemed at home in the tropics and barely survived the journey home when they left six months later.

'Joseph will get your baggage, and then we'll go home and have some cool drinks,' said Watson.

An African chauffeur, also in white suit and with a sun helmet at a rakish angle, ordered porters to take my goods to an old black Ford car at the back of the quay. We all got in, the Watsons at the back and myself in front with Joseph, who was a competent driver and all-job man.

Passing through Porto Novo town, we saw two- or three-storey shops and offices, bungalows and low houses, mud huts with rusty corrugated iron roofs, and wayside stalls. There were few tall buildings at that time, but there were some once-fine houses with verandas, shutters and interior courtyards of old Portuguese style. These had been copied from buildings of the first traders from the sixteenth century who, when this place was on the coast, had given it the name of New Port.

Now the whole town had an air of depression and neglect, and it was oppressively hot and damp. The elegant coconut palms of the sandy coast were replaced, even between the houses, by straight and squat oil palm trees, which were also spread over the countryside beyond. These trees were now the riches of Dahomey, planted to provide trade in palm oil after the suppression of the slave trade, but the trees were unattractive and many looked half decayed.

Porto Novo was the administrative capital of the whole French colony of Dahomey. Originally it had been an independent kingdom, known to most of its inhabitants as Hogbonou, or Ajashé in the Yoruba language, and it was wedged between the ancient Abomey and Yoruba western Nigeria. Being officially the head of Dan-homé, it was still 'the belly of Dan', the python. The snake symbol could be seen painted on houses or carved in wood, here and elsewhere. The serpent swallowing its own tail was a symbol of eternity, without beginning or end. The entire colony had been called Dahomey, but it is curious that the French retained the old English spelling of the name, with 'y' instead of an accented vowel. If the later name of Bénin is ever changed back, perhaps the accentuation may be changed also.

The Watsons lived in half of a fine new concrete house, beyond the main college buildings, and for a time I was lodged in the other half, which was occupied by the college principal, Herbert Bishop, and his wife, when they returned from furlough in December. Unfortunately, they, like the Watsons, were invalided home the next year, 1934, and I came back from the Ivory Coast to become principal at Porto Novo Seminary in 1937.

The Watsons were helpful and I took my main meals with them until the end of 1933. There were no difficulties with government officials, but I can anticipate here what happened when Mary and I arrived in Porto Novo, newly wed, in 1936.

* * * * *

We had travelled, as before, on a German launch from Lagos and spent the night at the frontier. We were met at Porto Novo wharf by a Swiss colleague, Paul Hoffer, who was due to go on leave but was living for the time being in our designated church house in the Ataké quarter to the north of Porto Novo town. Until he left, we were to be lodged in the larger of two flats over the main college buildings.

'My wife has got you some food in,' said Paul, 'and there is a cook who has prepared cold drinks and breakfast. I will leave you to unpack your goods and no doubt you will need a rest. I have to take the car to visit a village some miles away, but I shall be back by dark or shortly after. If you want anything, one of the boys, or a college student, can guide you to my house and my wife will help you. It is only a short walk away. Goodbye, Monsieur.'

Hoffer never called me by my Christian name, even later; nor did Watson, who used the surname, without Monsieur. There was much more formality in those days, and we only used Christian names with Ernest Taylor in 1939-40. With others, men and women, it was formality.

My wife and I settled in at the college flat, had a meal and unpacked essentials, remembering that we would be moving to the Ataké house before long. After an early lunch we went to the bedroom for a long overdue sleep, stripped and tried to get cool in a room darkened by shutters.

About four o'clock there was a sound of clapping, the way in which people announced visits. There was a bang at the door below and a shout of

'Police'. I got up from a heavy sleep and, shading my eyes, looked out of the window to see two Dahomean police in uniform in the college garden below.

'What is it? Is it me you wish?' I asked in halting French.

'Monsieur et Madame Pariser? You are to come at once to the police station.'

'What for?'

'I cannot say. The Chief Commissioner wishes to interview you both.'

'Is it far? We have no car.'

'It is two kilometres. You must walk. Come on, it is urgent.'

We dressed quickly and set off with the policemen along sandy lanes, stepping over open drains, and passing the mud and concrete houses of the town. We were soon wet with perspiration from the late afternoon sun and the humidity. It was stifling between the houses, with pungent smells from cooking pots and from large earthen containers of indigo dyes. Mary was new to Africa, understood little French, and was confused by the strange environment and the call to the police station. I could not explain it but was apprehensive.

The Police Commissariat was a long wooden building, alongside a rough road and facing a grassy bank which sloped down to the lagoon. There were people standing in groups outside or sitting on the grass, and they gazed curiously at two white people being escorted into the police station.

We were shown into an office, where there was a strong smell of alcohol. The commissioner was a tall swarthy Corsican, with flushed eyes and red nose, dressed in uniform. He kept us waiting for some minutes, strode in without introducing himself or offering to shake hands in the normal French fashion, and burst into a tirade.

'You come into this country. You flout the regulations. You act as if you own the place, like all Messieurs les Anglo-Saxons. If I were to go to your

Nigeria and behave like that, I should be thrown into prison. I could do the same to you now. Prison, do you know that?'

He pushed his face towards us, and his foul breath and the heavy air of the room made us shrink. Mary did not understand much that was said or comprehend any reason for the shouting, but the smell of drink and the dark military atmosphere were alarming. I put my hand under her arm, drew back a little and addressed the police chief.

'May my wife sit down, please? It would be courteous. We were travelling all night, we are tired, and she is a stranger here.'

The chief glared and snorted. He nodded to a policeman and two chairs were quickly brought, but he only allowed Mary to sit.

'Will you please tell me what this is about?' I asked.

'You have broken the restrictions on movement,' replied the chief harshly.

'What restrictions?'

'Yellow fever. You came from Lagos. It is infected.'

'We did not know.'

'You arrived on the German launch. Everybody was told on landing.'

'I repeat, we did not know, we were not told.'

'An officer from the hospital was there, checking all the passengers.'

'He did not check us,' I affirmed. 'We were met by a colleague and his chauffeur.'

'A native? He would surely know. But they are all disobedient, they avoid the law. No doubt you too think you are above the law, in your English snobbism. But it will not work here.'

'I take exception to that.'

'Enough,' declared the chief. 'This is a French country and you will obey our laws. Now, you will go back to your house. You will both get under a mosquito net at once. You will stay there all night. My sergeant will accompany you, to make sure you do as you are told. He will inspect you under the mosquito net this evening, at six o'clock, at nine, at midnight, at three in the morning, at six, and before eight he will see you go to the hospital. The doctor there is very angry with you for breaking his regulations. He has accused me of slackness. You will report to him and follow the treatment he prescribes. Now, be off.'

We stumbled out of the police station in bewilderment. There had been words like 'prison' and 'hospital' which were threatening. But there was reassurance from the Dahomean sergeant.

'Don't be alarmed,' he said. 'I know your college, and my daughter is at the girls' school. I shall take you home in a police car, and you may rest in peace all night. You would be well advised to sleep under a mosquito net in any case, but you will not be disturbed. I will come before eight in the morning, but no doubt Monsieur Hoffer will take you to the hospital in the mission car. I shall call on him to give him the news.'

So it happened. Paul Hoffer was shocked to hear of our adventure, and reproached himself for leaving us without transport. Next morning he took us to the Porto Novo small military hospital. There was only one army doctor and there was some confusion when we showed him our inoculation certificates.

Yellow fever was indeed one of the greatest menaces to life in those days. Sometimes whole towns were isolated until the infection had passed, and there were numerous fatalities. For years experiments had been conducted to find a cure or protection against the fever, and we had some of the first trials. Before leaving England Mary and I had been to the Wellcome Bureau in Euston Road, London, to be inoculated against yellow fever. Mary had two syringefuls of serum in her abdomen and, because I was heavier at that time, I had three. The experience was not too painful but, having taken the train back home, we had difficulty in standing straight when we had to get out and, in bed at night, we could hardly bear a sheet on our tender bodies.

At Porto Novo I had looked out our certificates and presented them to the doctor at the hospital but he did not seem to be impressed. Either he did not understand English or he thought the inoculations were too experimental or doubtful. He spoke to us sternly about the need to obey his regulations and report to the hospital daily for a week, and then weekly for a further month.

In the second week the doctor asked for specimens of our stools. There was no obvious connection with yellow fever, and there was no pathologist at Porto Novo hospital, which was a small establishment catering for the basic needs of men in the local defence services and attending to civilians only for fever and minor emergencies. But samples were to be sent for analysis at the larger hospital at the neighbouring port of Cotonou.

The following week the doctor inquired, 'What domestic staff have you, Monsieur?'

'A cook and a houseboy,' I replied.

'I shall require specimens from them also. They may bring them down themselves.'

I obtained small empty cigarette tins, of the sort used for imported cigarettes, and explained to the servants what was needed. Next morning the houseboy went gaily off to hospital, steering his bicycle with one hand and holding the tins in the other.

We watched him uncertainly.

'I wonder if he understood what was needed,' I said. 'I told the cook in French to take specimens. They could hardly make a mistake, could they?'

Next day a hospital orderly brought a note, and I read, 'Your servant brought the wrong kind of specimen. Kindly ensure that he brings the correct material without delay.'

'Oh dear, he will think I make a mockery of him at the Cotonou hospital. Excuse me, he is rather blunt.'

'I thought the boy didn't understand,' said Mary, 'and he balanced the tins very carefully.'

34

'Now I shall have to speak more plainly, and think up some pidgin French, petit nègre.'

This was done, with gestures, specimens were sent and we heard no more from the doctor. When six weeks were up an orderly discharged us from further visits to hospital, and we assumed that health regulations had been fulfilled.

* * * * *

In the middle of the day the whole town seemed to go to sleep, nature settling down under heavy layers of heat and damp. The noise in the road outside the college lessened, women at wayside stalls ceased crying their wares, and even dogs and chickens stopped scurrying about and crouched under the shade of trees and houses.

We enjoyed our noontide rest and slowly became acclimatized. One afternoon we had gone to bed and lay undressed on top of a sheet on our double bed, a little apart to allow for air. A big mosquito net was wound up above us, the shutters were fastened and the atmosphere was close, but darkness seemed cooler than the glare outside.

In the quiet there came a knock at the door below and I awoke in confusion. I got up, slipped on my shorts, opened a shutter and called out, 'What do you want?'

'Police.'

'Oh, no. What is it this time?'

'The commissioner wishes to see you both, sir.'

'Then he can wait till I get the car.'

Hoffer had returned from travel and the mission car was in the garage in our college compound. I scribbled a note and sent it with the houseboy, while we got dressed. After a time Joseph, the chauffeur, came and we were driven with the policeman to the station.

There the commissioner greeted us with outstretched hand and himself got us both chairs. It was early for him and he had not had his lunch. He smiled and looked at us quizzically, as if wondering why we had come.

'Madame and Monsieur Pariser, I believe. It is good of you to visit me. I must return your call.'

'What is it this time?' I asked. 'We have not been out of Porto Novo, and we have completed the treatment at the hospital.'

'Of course. The doctor is quite pleased. He thanked me for my zeal. But I have nothing else for you.'

'That is not the impression I had. I thought by your urgent call that we had committed another crime, unwittingly.'

'Oh. Perhaps it is that stupid clerk. I mentioned that I needed to complete my records.'

'He sent an officer to call us, without delay.'

'These natives. They get everything wrong.'

'What, then, did you need for your records?' I asked.

'A mere detail,' he replied. 'It is Madame, if I may ask her.'

'If you will be precise, I will explain to her.'

'Of course. Madame, what was your mother's maiden name?'

'Your mother's maiden name?' I interpreted slowly.

'It was Baker,' she replied.

'Ah, Boulanger,' said the commissioner, showing that he knew some English, and he bowed.

'Is that all?' I asked coldly.

'That is all, Monsieur. My books must be complete, you understand. But do not deprive me of the pleasure of your company too quickly.'

'It is the heat of the day,' I pointed out. 'We were having our siesta.'

'Naturally. How thoughtless of that clerk. He shall be disciplined. Allow me, Madame.'

The commissioner rose, moved the chairs and showed us to the door. He shook hands firmly, bidding us farewell, with hopes that we might meet again soon.

We got into the car and went home in silence. When we reached the bedroom, we looked at each other at last, stripped and fell on the bed, helpless with laughter.

5. THE SEMINARY

Like many West African towns, Porto Novo had once been protected by a long mud wall, which formed almost a semi-circle to the north. In the thirties, fragments of this ancient wall were still to be seen in some places, though most of it had disappeared. The southern part of the town faced the lagoon, which served as a boundary and had given some protection in times of war.

The principal Protestant church, founded in 1862, was in the heart of the town, in the quarter of Ouézoumé, and in the thirties the mission house was by the north-eastern wall, near the ruins of Ataké gate, of which a few stumps remained. To the north there was cleared land and new buildings, including a large Protestant complex, consisting of a college or seminary, a new girls' school and eventually a new boys' school. Beyond that, round the outer side of the town, there was the Boulevard, a band of grass and trees, soon to be invaded by more buildings.

The Protestant college was an ambitious pile, a cement shell over sun-dried bricks, with twenty square pillars in front and the same number behind, lining verandas which led to half a dozen classrooms. In the central block was a large hall, used as a chapel on Sundays and divided into two or three classrooms during the week. Above this hall were living quarters, a large flat designed for a married couple and a small apartment for a single teacher. Facing the main building, like the top and bottom sections of an E-shape, were one-storey dormitories for the students.

The college looked out over a large garden and a small house for a junior teacher. At the end of the garden, a long and high concrete wall separated the college from a public road, which was usually noisy with traffic and lined with wayside stalls. The college was like a fortress over a peasant village.

This college had originally been planned, about 1920, as a boys' high school, on the pattern of the best schools in neighbouring Nigeria. Before the French conquest of Dahomey in 1894 mission school teaching had been partly in English, with small classes in mud huts. The original aim, as in other missions, had been to enable converts to read the Bible, but the curriculum was soon extended.

Porto Novo Seminary 1933
Institute of Theology 1999

In Nigeria, after the colonial scramble of the 1890s, mission schools, continuing with English and a fuller syllabus, were aided by government funds, since they were cheap substitutes for official schools. Indeed, both government offices and, later, the universities, would have been impossible without the education given by the mission schools to students and would-be clerks.

On the French side, things were more difficult for a mission of British origin. The English language was forbidden, first by custom and then formally. No financial grants were given to mission schools, as the government preferred to run its own small but select schools. Indeed, no educational subsidies were given to either Catholic or Protestant schools in French Territories until after the Second World War. Even where mission schools struggled on, French qualifications were insisted upon for teachers, and the syllabus that applied throughout France was imposed.

'The geography of France at nine every Monday morning, from Paris to Porto Novo, and the history of France at ten, from Caen to Cotonou,' complained a teacher. 'There is no adaptation to different hours or climate.'

In the twenties, the plans for a boys' high school or college in Porto Novo were complicated by developments in French-speaking territories elsewhere. A mass movement to Christianity in the French Ivory Coast, sparked by a Liberian prophet, William Wadé Harris in 1913, had led to appeals for French-speaking missionaries, ministers and catechists, and in 1924 a number had gone from Dahomey and Togo. This movement and its development will be mentioned again later (chapter 13), but it had an immediate effect on proposals for a college in Porto Novo.

French-speaking minister-teachers, British and French, had been recruited for the Porto Novo college. But from the Ivory Coast it soon became clear that training was desperately needed for African leaders, ministers and catechists. A catechist school was opened at Dabou in the Ivory Coast, and the college at Porto Novo was abandoned as a school and changed into a training place for catechists and pastors. It was given the new title of Séminaire to indicate its character, and the minister-teachers either became local pastors or went to the Ivory Coast as evangelists.

When I arrived in 1933, the Porto Novo institution, no longer a school or lay college, was a Séminaire flourishing in theological training, with students from three French colonies, Dahomey, Togo and Ivory Coast. This theological teaching has lasted some seventy years and it still continues today in the Institute of Theology in Porto Novo.

Various tales were told of previous teachers at the Porto Novo Seminary. There was one muscular Christian who showed a fortress mentality. Unlike most missionaries, who did not hunt, he had a hunting gun. He took it down off the wall where it was hanging, and offered it to one of the Demoiselles from the girls' school so that she could feel its weight.

'No, thank you,' she said, recoiling. 'What are you going to do with that thing? There is no hunting round here. The farmers have long since killed or chased away the large wild animals, and they cultivate all the land between the oil palms.'

'This is my burglary insurance,' he replied grimly. 'There have been several break-ins near the Seminary recently and the local police do nothing. Even the so-called 'secret societies' make a lot of noise but seem to catch nobody. I shall see what a little godly fear will do.'

The concrete wall at the end of the grounds was visible from the upper flats, especially on moonlit nights, and this man watched in the dusk for intruders. One night, hearing a shout of 'voleurs' (thieves) from the secret society, he took down his gun. Thinking he could discern a figure scrambling over the wall, he fired into the dark. Then was a grunt, then silence.

'I don't know whether I winged him, or he just fell off in fright,' he said, 'but there have been no thieves since in our grounds. This must be fearsome taboo.'

* * * * *

The principal's house, where the Watsons, the Bishops and later my wife and I lived, has already been mentioned. It was a two-storey concrete building, with a corrugated asbestos roof, erected about 1930, in two sections. Each had cement floors downstairs, and wooden floors, which were kept polished, upstairs. From the ground level wooden stairs led up to a large lounge, a double bedroom to the right, a small dressing-room and a bathroom. There was some local and some imported furniture, the latter chiefly a dressing-table with a large mirror, and a fine wardrobe. I lived there for three months in 1933, Mary and I from 1937 to 1940, and I again in 1945-6. When the veteran French missionary Paul Wood and his wife were there in 1941-5, they installed a punkah in the dining-room, a wide cloth fan pulled by a small boy sitting on the verandah outside, but we took it down when they left.

Although the seminary living apartments were all good and modern, there was no running water. Cooks or houseboys, therefore, had to draw water from a deep communal college well between the principal's house and the main buildings. Bathrooms contained low round zinc baths and wash-basins, but all water, cold and hot, had to be carried upstairs in old square petrol cans. Water was heated over wood fires on kitchen ranges. We installed a full-size bath in 1938, but water still had to be carried up to it, and a drain made to empty it.

In the flats over the two main seminary buildings small bathrooms were fitted up on the wide back verandas, surrounded by wooden partitions, open at the top. It was said that a visiting important secretary from London was taking his tub there when a bat flew over the partition and settled on his head. He seized it, opened the door and threw it out. But the bat came back over the partition and sat on his head again. This earned a bad mark for the staff when he went back home. Later we met this secretary on a visit to West Africa and took him round some of the villages. But when, on leave, we called on him at the London office, he hardly remembered us and was full of his own importance, since on a visit to India he had been called 'bishop'.

Bats flew everywhere at night, coming in from the bush at dusk like black flying armies. Although the seminary houses were well built, bats found their way in between the ceilings and the roofs where some of them sheltered in the daytime. The ceilings were made of asbestos squares, and during the night bats could be clearly heard, sliding over the squares and giving nightmares to some of the sleepers in the bedrooms below. Every so often we sent the college guardian or the chauffeur up into the lofts of the houses and the seminary dormitories, to knock down bats which hung from the rafters. They were put in pails and buried in the communal midden. Once the chauffeur, balancing on the rafters, slipped and put his foot through an asbestos square. In the bedroom below his black foot and leg appeared. Fortunately, he was only scratched but he drove himself to hospital, had his wound dressed, and was out of action for a week.

Lizards ran in and out of the houses and classrooms, grey females with orange-headed males chasing them. Little geckos, with suckers on their feet, ran up walls and over ceilings and sometimes dropped down on tables or floors. Flying ants came occasionally in swarms and had to be swept away. Mosquitoes were ever-present and we would go round with folded newspapers to hit them and, if lucky, leave a ring of our blood on the wall. The inter-denominational paper, the *British Weekly*, was just the right weight to swat mosquitoes. Once, after very heavy rain, our house was surrounded with water and toads came out croaking noisily, until the soft red earth absorbed the waters.

With no running water there were no flush lavatories. There were 'thunder boxes', in small rooms with trap doors, with pails which were emptied at night by Kiti, the seminary guardian. He did the round of the houses in the dark, with a cloth over his face, to collect the pails one by one and bury the refuse in the garden.

There was an erratic electricity supply from Porto Novo town. It usually came on at dusk, about six in the evening, often went off for short or long periods, and finished around ten. We kept in reserve pressure lamps and storm lanterns, such as were used up country at Dassa and elsewhere. There was no refrigerator. Some foods were kept in a small safe with a metal grille, its feet being stood in little pots of paraffin to prevent ants getting at the food. Tinned butter was put in a large thermos flask with lumps of ice. The ice was obtained from the railway station down by the lagoon, and our cook rode down the two miles on his bicycle to fetch the ice, which he brought back in a small sack, dripping on the road. Drinking water was taken from the well, boiled and put in a filter. A smaller filter was taken on trek to villages where water was often cloudy or brown.

* * * * *

One of the teachers, an excellent French speaker, was restless, impatient and intolerant of mistakes. He was insistent on names, rebuking late-comers harshly and carrying an alarm clock, which he set for the exact end of each hour, into class. He expected his colleagues to observe precise time, too, and was cross if he was kept waiting for another class to end. Not surprisingly, the students tried to keep other teachers talking, so as to delay the start of the next lesson, and this annoyed him.

This teacher towered over his pupils as he walked to and fro on a little platform in front of a blackboard. He used chalk freely to write names and draw diagrams, and chalk was his favourite weapon for waking any who were nodding off in the heat of the afternoon. Not a good shot, he threw hard but often wide of his targets.

One day he had used up all his chalk when he spotted a student sinking his head into his arms. He seized the clock and hurled it at the sleeper. Luckily he missed, and the clock crashed to pieces against a wall. The pupils looked at him with fear, but in frustration he tore off his own glasses, threw them to the ground and stamped on them. He could not see without them, and stumbled from the class to his own quarters. Then a telegram had to be sent to his home in Lancashire for new glasses, and he had to stay in his room, fiddling with papers and unable to teach for a month, till the new spectacles came out by post.

43

The seminary garden was an oasis between college buildings and the stores and huts of the town beyond. Further on there were monotonous fields of maize, cassava and oil palms that filled the countryside. This extensive garden had been planted under the direction of previous occupiers with flowering bougainvillaea, frangipani, oleander, bushes of various coloured croton leaves, and many roses and other flowering shrubs. There were fruit trees of guava, mango, orange, lemon, citron, banana, pawpaw and pomegranate; also oil, coconut and traveller's palm trees, and plantations of pineapple, cassava and groundnuts. At night we could sometimes hear guava fruit falling to the ground as bats fed on them.

The grounds were easily overgrown and needed constant tending, for in the damp heat weeds seemed to sprout overnight and soon became tangled thickets. Small gardens round the teachers' houses were kept tidy, but occasionally workmen were brought in. Then it was decided that this was wasteful and that students should be called on to make their surroundings a weed-free showpiece.

It was decreed that pupils should do manual work, to make a healthy break from classes. But the students seemed only to want to study. Unlike most European pupils they preferred study even to games, and some of them appeared to think that gardening was beneath the dignity of catechists or pastors who were proficient in French language and literature, as well as theology and philosophy. Consequently, if they did weeding, it was often in a casual manner that irritated the supervising teachers who did not know how to force them to work harder.

The students were watched and chivvied at manual work ('travail manuel'), which became part of the seminary timetable and which, among themselves, was known as 'forced labour'. The French government imposed forced labour on people in the villages who tried to avoid paying taxes, and sometimes rows of these unwilling workers could be seen walking in file along the roads, roped together, neck to neck, men, women and children, and guarded by African soldiers with rifles, to the shame of their fellows.

College manual work was nothing like that, and teachers often worked alongside students, since some of them liked gardening and did not mind getting their hands dirty. But it was exhausting work in the heat, even in the slightly cooler times before sunset; and if hands or legs were scratched with thorns, the wounds easily turned septic.

* * * * *

Varieties of food provided further grounds for conflict. At first students cooked their own meals and ate them on the wide verandas outside their dormitories. But these became greasy and untidy, and we decided to have a refectory built on spare land behind the first dormitory. This was a concrete shelter with a corrugated iron roof, open at the sides, and fitted with tables, benches and a small kitchen. A cook was employed, and a healthy menu worked out. But there were problems. Students came from different towns and villages in Dahomey, Togo and the Ivory Coast. There were varying tribal customs, not least where food was concerned, and a deputation waited on us.

'Please, sir, I cannot eat yam,' said one.

'We have a taboo on cassava,' said another.

'My father forbade me to eat plantain,' added a third.

We talked it over with European and African teachers and called a meeting of the leading students.

'These food taboos are superstitions which educated men ought to have outgrown and Christian students should reject,' we said. 'Our funds are limited and we cannot provide for every fancy.'

'Then we cannot eat,' answered the students. 'We hear that in Europe there is a thing called "strike". We will strike on your food, and each one cook his own, as we did before.'

'What do we do now?' we asked our African colleagues.

'Your predecessor said that if they did not eat, they should not be taught.'

'A lock-out. The classic response. Do you agree?'

'No. Education is scarce in this country, and the church would suffer. Moreover, to be deprived of teaching would be a blow not only to learning but also to pride. It would cause resentment that might last a long time. Our men are needed urgently in the churches, and the Chairman of the mission would probably not allow us to close down.'

'Then we must compromise. The students are not unreasonable, and normally they are well behaved and respectful. If they will accept some agreed foods, learn from each other, attend classes and do some gardening, then we will ask the cook to provide more variety. There may be alternative dishes, as much as he can manage within our limited budget.'

This was agreed. The very next morning the reading in chapel was, 'Let not him that eats, despise him that eats not,' and we all laughed.

* * * * *

The syllabus for teaching catechists and ministers was roughly based on patterns of theological training in Britain, with a strong emphasis on Old and New Testament study. All the students were literate in French, which was essential for members of different tribal groups and languages, and was required by the government. But advanced French was taught, with language and literature, and French and African history and geography. Instruction was also given in church history, liturgy and organization, with special attention to French Protestantism and to Methodism, which at the time had separate churches in France.

Two things were lacking: knowledge of the African church background, by most teachers, and acquaintance with traditional African religion. A succession of teachers had come from Europe, mainly Britain and France, but with some Swiss and Dutch. At first they knew only of the European patterns of life and teaching, but some contacts with the local church began as they settled in. There was regular attendance at the main Protestant church in Porto Novo, which will have its own chapter next. And visits were encouraged at weekends to village chapels, in the sandy stretches of the Atlantique seaboard region, and to villages in the interior at Adjarra,

Méridjonou and beyond. I was sent for three months to work in Porto Novo towns and villages, and later to Dassa Zoumé up country.

The African minister on our teaching staff, Paul Hountodji, was the only one of us who knew Dahomean church life from the inside, for he had been a catechist and teacher before his ministerial training. He necessarily took the classes in pastoral theology and African church history. Paul was very short, barely up to my shoulder, and when we were photographed side by side, in large white sun helmets, we looked an odd couple.

African indigenous religion was all around us in Dahomey, but little seemed to have been done to understand or study it. As a result, it was brushed aside or condemned out of hand as 'fetish' or 'gris-gris'. It certainly did not appear as a subject in the curriculum. Yet, occasionally, some of the students betrayed, by word or attitude, a little of the powerful background from which they had partly emerged. A chapter will be devoted to this religion later.

Books for theological study were all in French, though some students had begun to study English, thereby gaining access to much more Protestant literature, and those from Togo might have a German background, as it had been a German colony with Lutheran missions before 1918. French books were nearly all published in paperback, even the large and invaluable commentaries by Père Lagrange on the Gospels. Yet at that time paperbacks were frowned on by the British, as inferior and the sort of thing that the French did. The first appearance of paperback Penguin Books, at sixpence each, was in 1935.

At the seminary we decided that it would be helpful for the students, and provide practical exercise, if their textbooks could be bound. So we got manuals on bookbinding, ordered some materials from England, and asked a local church carpenter to make a wooden binding frame. This work became very popular, and most students managed to bind some of the more used or expensive books. Sixty years on I still have a few self-bound books from Porto Novo.

* * * * *

The countless early deaths of Europeans, recorded in the first years of West African missions, led to the building of fine spacious houses, far removed from the mud huts of pioneer days. They were luxurious compared with many houses in Porto Novo town, and with those of African junior staff. In addition to their salaries, missionaries had many allowances, for furniture, household fittings and linen, travel and children's education at boarding schools in Europe.

When I went to the university in Nigeria later, the mission house secretary in London wrote to say that, since my salary was higher than that of an ordinary missionary, I should pay part of it to the society. I went down to Lagos to see the chairman, Alan Angus, and together we worked out that although my basic university salary was larger, the allowances for rent, travel, and especially children's education were less. Overall, missionaries did as well as university lecturers. And there had been no recognition of the great personal expenses I had had over the years, for books, examination fees and writing materials, which had gained me the university post.

In the thirties and forties, houses for African teachers and ministers were usually smaller than those of missionaries. At the Porto Novo seminary, for example, the sole African teacher lived in a bungalow at the end of the college grounds, near the wall which separated it from the public highway. It was a small building, where Paul Hountodji was lodged with his wife and family.

Paul was a helpful colleague, modest, with a slight lisp, and always deferentially saying 'Monsieur'. In 1933 I could not invite him to a meal, since I was eating with the Watsons, and in those days in Dahomey it was unheard of to have an African to dinner, even a minister of the church. Later on Mary did have his wife and child to tea. It was assumed that there was no colour bar, but in fact it existed in things not done, and in a separation of living conditions which was real, though on our side almost unnoticed.

Colour distinctions were as evident among the French as with the British, and they were increased by the habit of some French speakers in addressing all Africans, even ministers of the church, with the familiar 'tu', used for children and servants in France. Some of us tried using 'vous' for servants, but wondered if it was not too ostentatious. Again, it was only after the war, and at university, that hospitality between races and colours was open and prejudices were overcome, almost.

Staff and students at Porto Novo Seminary 1940
Front row: Mary Parrinder, Geoffrey Parrinder, Ernest Taylor, Moïse Sagbohan

Teaching in French, not the native language of either teacher or pupils, though the latter were sometimes the more fluent, was a strange experience. The students were young men, of varying shades of colour, and a very dark man might be called 'that black one'. They mostly wore open-necked khaki shirts, shorts and sandals, and sandals were slipped off during lessons and toes wiggled. Sometimes they wiped their pens in their thick black curly hair, and the violet ink had no obvious effect. But ministerial students generally wore long trousers, and at times jackets and ties. When ordained, they wore clerical collars, though we exhorted them to adapt dress from local customs, with long white or blue robes. But when we suggested discarding the dog-collar, they protested, 'Our people will say we curse them, sir.'

Most of the students were intelligent, the élite of the churches, keen to learn and follow the latest in theological debate. It was the time of the dominance of Karl Barth and his dogmatic teachings, but we tried to temper this influence with the criticisms of Bultmann and Brunner. There were some French translations of the relevant books, but much depended on interpretations by teachers, who might or might not share their views.

49

French Protestants, as I had found during a year at the theological faculty at Montpellier, were divided between traditionalists and liberals. Methodists in France tended to be 'traditional', but this did not necessarily apply to those from Britain.

There was a small number of Dahomean catechist students, as well as ministerial, at Porto Novo in 1933, and more came from the Ivory Coast in 1936, including some I had taught in the meantime at the Dabou seminary. Although travel was difficult between the Ivory Coast and Dahomey during the war, in the period of the German-dominated Vichy government in France, some communications were maintained, and a succession of students at Porto Novo underwent both catechist and ministerial training.

Catechists were the great unsung workers of the churches. Unlike most missionaries, they spoke the language of the people, from whom they came and to whom they were still close; and they knew far more of church life than any missionary. Though poorly paid, they both ran the village churches and frequently pioneered work in new areas. They were the true 'missionaries'.

Ordinary church members included preachers and Sunday School teachers, and they and many others took their position and religion seriously. When, in the seventies, church schools in Dahomey were taken over for a time by the Communist government and religious instruction was forbidden by the Marxists, Dahomean church leaders and members met their children coming out of school and took them home or to church for religious lessons.

It was a sign of the long-established church in Dahomey that three ministers had been newly trained at the end of 1933, and of its limited range that no more candidates appeared for several years. Paul Hountodji was stationed at the seminary, Georges Gbeyongbé was placed at the Porto Novo church but under the superintendence of a younger missionary, Paul Hoffer from Switzerland. The third, John Kpomegbé, went to his native Togo, under the oversight of newly-arrived Henri James from Holland.

At that time, there were only nine or ten African Methodist ministers, with the same number of European missionaries, for the whole of Dahomey-Togo. But by 2000, despite the interlude of Marxist anti-religious government, there were over forty African church ministers in the country, some of them my own students, and nearly all foreign missionaries had left.

50

6. OUÉZOUMÉ CHURCH

In the 1930s, the principal Protestant church in Porto Novo was already past its third generation and has now had its centenary. Its members, proud of their Christian history, did not regard us as missionaries to them, but as doing the special work of education and leadership training. There are still many non-Christians in Dahomey-Bénin, and their evangelization is the task of the local church, which has made big advances in recent times.

In the early years of the nineteenth century missionaries of various societies were seeking to penetrate West Africa and often dying in the attempt because of the malarial climate. Thomas Birch Freeman, however, the coloured son of a negro father and an English mother, was able to withstand the climate, and he visited many of the old African kingdoms, from Kumasi in 1839 to Abomey, and in 1842 from Badagry to Abeokuta.

It was from Badagry in 1862 that an African minister, Thomas J. Marshall, who was the son of a priest of the traditional religion named Kakpo, came to found a church in Porto Novo. He asked King Sodji of Porto Novo for land, near a temple of the snake god Dangbé, in the Ouézoumé (Way-Zoom-May) quarter of the town, which was named after the village from which the snake-cult came. The chief of that quarter opposed the request but was overruled, and Marshall built the first small church there.

Marshall converted one of the court ministers, Sotin, and strengthened his position. Sotin, though attracting some of his colleagues to the Protestant church on Sundays, continued, despite his conversion, to perform the ritual ceremonies of the old religion, consulting the oracle Fa and offering annual sacrifices. Then a new king, Mikpon, demanded that Sotin renounce the Christian religion. Marshall was thrown into prison and his flock dispersed, and Sotin went into exile to relieve the pressure.

After a short time Thomas Marshall was released and Christian services were re-established in Porto Novo, continuing with small numbers for the rest of the century. Marshall died in 1899 and his grave in the grounds of the large modern church is still revered.

Christian religious instruction in Porto Novo had been undertaken by a catechist, Frederick Martins, who held classes in a little hut every Sunday.

51

Martins was later ordained as a minister, and after Marshall's death he succeeded him in charge of the church.

It was Wesleyan Methodism from Britain that was established in Porto Novo, and when French rule came in the nineties, it was the only Protestant mission to be given official recognition in Dahomey. Probably the Methodists would have preferred British rule, with the incorporation of Porto Novo into Nigeria, but it was not to be.

There were generally good relations with the Anglican Church Missionary Society in Nigeria, and when Anglicans and members of other Protestant churches came to Porto Novo they usually attended worship at Ouézoumé. There arose, however, several breakaway independent African churches, which will be mentioned later.

* * * * *

As early as 1660, Spanish Capuchins established a Roman Catholic mission in the town of Allada, between Abomey and coastal Whydah (Ouidah). The mission was short-lived, but its *Doctrina Christiana,* translated into the Fon language, has been preserved in Madrid, and was reprinted in Paris in 1929.

Roman Catholic priests arrived in Porto Novo in 1864, two years after Thomas Marshall. Having been given hospitality by the king, they asked after a time for land on which to build their church. There was some opposition, and they were offered a site in thick forest to the west of the town which was supposed to be haunted by evil spirits. It was hoped that the demons would chase the Catholics away, but a small chapel was built on a rubbish dump at the foot of a giant silk-cotton tree. Although the country might easily have passed under British rule, a French school was opened in 1865 and provided the first native civil servants after the French occupation. By 1930 a large Roman Catholic cathedral, in yellow and pink stucco, was in full use.

* * * * *

52

In 1933 the Ouézoumé church building was fairly large, about 100 feet long by 50 wide. It was built of sun-dried bricks, covered with cement and pink-washed. Indoors the walls were whitewashed, and there were wooden doors and black painted shutters for windows. Outside there was an open compound surrounded by a low wall. At the top end were the graves of Marshall and Martins, and a bell hanging between two concrete pillars to announce the times of services. In the quiet of early morning, in Lent and Advent, the bell, summoning the faithful to the crowded daily prayers at six o'clock, could be heard a mile away in the mission house at Ataké.

The church was full of wooden pews in the central section and at each side beyond the aisles. In the front centre was a large wooden rostrum, communion table and pulpit. At one side were pews for missionaries and teachers, and at the other side pews for church elders. A gallery above and behind the pulpit was for the harmonium and organist, and for the choir of men and boys in black cassocks and white surplices. Behind the end wall was a small vestry for the clergy, the choir having to assemble in the compound outside and then mount by a staircase to the gallery.

At eight o'clock on Sunday mornings the first warning bell was tolled for five minutes, to be followed at half past by regular ringing and at five to nine by quieter ringing still. Services began at nine o'clock, more or less, but people came in and out of the doors at various times. The windows were usually wide open, but during tornadoes, when they were closed, rain rattled noisily on the corrugated iron roof and the heat and darkness increased. The church was usually full on ordinary Sundays, and with large blocks from the schools and seminary, it was already clear that a great new cathedral, which now exists, would have to be planned.

At special times, Easter, Whitsun, Harvest, Christmas and New Year, the congregation overflowed into the compound outside and many people crowded round the windows to get a look in, different classes taking it in turns to find reserved places.

People put on their best clothes for church. Some women wore European-style dresses and hats, especially those whose families came from long-established churches in Sierra Leone, and they frowned on bare heads or scarves as 'bush' dress. Sunday required straw hats, the more decorated the better. But most local women had coloured scarves and patterned blouses and skirts. Popular in 1933 were the newly-arrived printed cloths with pictures of the centenary of the abolition of the slave trade, probably made in Manchester. Educated men often wore white suits, and others plain robes. The more elaborate Yoruba and Hausa-style robes of later nationalistic dress had hardly appeared yet. Children were dressed in their best, and girls and women had spent many painful hours on Saturday having their curly hair tightly bound in squares, lines and other patterns.

There was only one mission car in Porto Novo at that time, under the control of the superintendent minister of the circuit who lived in the Ataké house, and he loaned it out for shopping and other needs as requested. So on Sunday mornings most of us from the seminary and schools walked the mile down to Ouézoumé. The men were in white suits and sun helmets, with leather shoes or sometimes plimsolls. The ladies wore short-sleeved dresses, perhaps with stockings, with sun helmets or double felt hats, and sometimes carried sunshades.

It was already hot at eight thirty, and patches of sweat appeared under the arms and down the backs of the clothes of the most dignified ladies or gentlemen. The path – hardly a road, though used for carts – was of red earth, with gullies for the rain. It went between mud houses and concrete shops, passing near an Independent Church, which was ignored. About halfway there was a clearing for the indigo-dyers, with tall earthen pots and dark blue cloths stretched out over the ground to dry, all giving off a pungent smell. At the church compound we went through the gate, round the back to the vestry and on to reserved seats at the front of the church, which was already crowded, hot and noisy.

As the church was of the old Wesleyan tradition the order of Morning Prayer was used, from the Anglican *Book of Common Prayer*. This suited Anglican visitors from Nigeria and the Gold Coast, though it was strange to missionaries from continental Reformed or Lutheran traditions. There were occasional Greek Orthodox visitors from Greek shops in the town, and they said they preferred these services to those of Roman Catholics, where much was in Latin.

Our services were mostly conducted in the local language, Goungbé or Allada, and the liturgy had been translated from the Prayer Book many years before. French versions of the Prayer Book, coming from a rather stilted translation made for the Anglican Church in French-speaking parts of Canada, were used at times. In the missionary pews there were several copies of the Authorized Version of the English Bible, with the preface to 'the most high and mighty Prince James, King of Great Britain, France and Ireland', and we delighted in pointing this out to our republican French colleagues.

Canticles, psalms and hymns had been translated and duly took their place, though they were sung with more zeal than understanding. For we soon realised that Goungbé, like many African languages, was tonal, with rising and falling inflexions. But the hymns and psalms were set to tunes imported from Europe or America, classical or Victorian church music, and Moody and Sankey compositions.

It followed inevitably that musical intonations could not fit the spoken language, and frankly made nonsense of the words. That church congregations sang and persevered with this incomprehensible production was more a tribute to their fidelity to the customs of their forebears than to real participation and enjoyment. Any outsider, speaking the Goun language, would have been completely at a loss to understand the words. There were a few local songs, looked down on as choruses, and only decades later were attempts made to compose and use Christian hymns in different languages and tunes of Africa.

The church services were conducted, sometimes in relays, by African ministers and lay preachers, but there might be a sermon by a colleague, and this was what chiefly interested us. If the service was entirely in a local language, we might prefer to give it a miss and await the evening seminary chapel service, which was always in French.

In theory missionaries should learn the language of the country, but few of those engaged in teaching had the time or inclination to pick up more than a few common phrases and greetings. Only those involved in church work up country, and not many of them, became at all fluent in an African language. Nevertheless we tried some language study. I had been told not to learn Goungbé, since others were supposed to be doing that, but to study Yoruba, which was the language of western Nigeria next door and many Porto Novians spoke it. I had three months' Yoruba lessons from a student, then moved to the Ivory Coast to learn Adjoukrou at Dabou, on after a year to Avikam at Grand Lahou, back to Dassa in Dahomey for a dialect of Yoruba, and at last more general Yoruba at Ibadan in Nigeria. But in Dahomey and the Ivory Coast, French was my African language for teaching and preaching, used far more than other Europeans practised with any indigenous African language.

At my first service at Ouézoumé, John Watson gave the sermon. He was dressed in a white suit and clerical collar, as were the African ministers present. Three years later, when I was in charge of the Porto Novo circuit for a time, I began to wear a black Geneva gown over a white suit, and was probably the first European minister to do so in Dahomey. Church leaders at once congratulated me on this dress, and next Sunday African ministers came out in their own gowns, which they already possessed and wore when Europeans were not present. They loved elaborate clothes, and in later times went in for many varieties of costume. Exiled to Cornwall during the war, I may also have been the first minister to wear a gown in those old-fashioned chapels. In Nigeria later we had white cassocks made, which was an innovation for Methodists and Presbyterians, though not for other churches.

Watson's sermon was a textual exposition, short and in formal French. But its length was more than doubled by the interpretation. An African interpreter put it, sentence by sentence, into Goungbé, and sometimes there was a second translation into Yoruba. Whether Goungbé is a more flowery language than French or not, it went on longer, and sometimes one suspected that the interpreter, or 'interrupter', might be saying something like, 'I don't know what this white man means, but this is what you ought to hear.'

With the full order of Morning Prayer, hymns, psalms, canticles, lessons, creed, prayers, sermon, announcements and collections, we were lucky to get away under two hours. There were sometimes two or three collections of money, taken in large bags and presented and blessed with ceremony. During the hymns stewards walked slowly up and down the aisles, counting the numbers present and noting them in books, and the numbers would be announced the following Sunday, along with the amount of the offerings. Also, during the sermon and interpretations, stewards with rods would walk along the aisles, to quieten any crying child and waken, with a prod in the ribs, any worshipper who was nodding off or had fallen asleep.

Services, despite length and dreary patches, were good-humoured. After the last blessings members would come to shake hands, parents making sure that they greeted teachers at the girls' school, who were great favourites. If we tried to push our way through to the main doors, there would be many to salute us, and always the stewards with firm handshakes.

On the second Sunday there were baptisms of children. A row of mothers sat in the front pews, in best outfits but with blouses pulled up to suckle the babies. Babies were rushed out if they cried too much, but ministers handled them professionally for sprinkling in baptism. For adult baptisms Pentecost (Whitsun) was the great occasion, with all the male and female candidates dressed in white. The service was even longer than usual, but happy and good-tempered.

The third Sunday after my arrival was the Harvest Festival. It was in October, following European custom, though harvests in Africa were at different times of the year. The church was full well before nine, and it was lavishly decorated with flowers, fruit, flags and streamers. When we arrived on time there was hardly room to squeeze in, and we went out when possible for a break and a drink of squash, brought by those who were in the know, in the vestry. People crowded in the compound outside and leant at the windows.

The service began as usual with the full order of Morning Prayer, followed by sermons in French, Goungbé and perhaps Yoruba, but that was only the start. The central activities on this day were presentations of gifts, of fruit, cloth or money. Different organizations of the church and its leaders took part: preachers, stewards, Leaders, Sunday School classes, membership classes, and many others. Each group brought its own harvest gift. Often all members were in similar costumes, and as some people belonged to several groups, they would go out and change dress before the next presentation. Up one aisle they went in uniform, singing a special hymn and walking or jogging pace by pace. At the front they presented their gifts, received a blessing from one of the ministers, and slowly retired, singing, down the other aisle, while the next group entered by the first door.

We escaped about midday, soaked with sweat, and walked back home in the heat. Energetic ones might go back for the afternoon service, which went on till dusk.

On the Monday evening there was a sale of goods, to which we might go down. From twilight people began to fill the grounds of the church, where lanterns and little clay lamps were put on tables and stands. There were electric lights but the supply was unreliable. Other tables held cloths, fruit, vegetables, and various items for sale. A band of drummers was already active, but the sale began well after dark. It was an auction sale, people bidding one against another, to raise as much money as possible for church funds and projects.

The sale went on for several hours, and refreshments were served of tea, orange squash and palm wine. This last was not approved by some of the Europeans, and even less the dancing that followed. But both were old and popular customs, and they would be taken up again when the visitors had gone.

At New Year's Eve there was a great Watchnight service, with a crowded church overflowing into the compound outside. Fireworks and guns were fired off after the striking of midnight.

7. INDEPENDENCY AND ISLAM

Although the Methodist Church was the only Protestant body recognized by the French government of Dahomey, there existed other unregistered Christian groups, local Independents or Nonconformists. Independent or prophetical 'sects', separate from the main mission or official organizations, are a widespread phenomenon in modern Africa, and thousands of them have been studied and described throughout the continent.

I had various opportunities of exploring the highways and byways of the rambling old town of Porto Novo, and of visiting the Independents, and researches were conducted in 1936 and again in 1945. I found seven such churches, and no doubt there are now many more, since their numbers have increased almost everywhere in Africa. In 1955 I identified more such communities in the Nigerian city of Ibadan, and recorded them in my book, *Religion in an African City*. Thanks to later charismatic movements and television evangelists, such religions have proliferated further.

The Independents I identified at Porto Novo in the thirties and forties were: African Bethel, Eleja Methodist, Cherubim and Seraphim, Christianisme Céleste, Christique, Église des Oracles, and Orunmila, and they fell roughly into three categories. The first two may be called 'orthodox', since in the main they followed the worship and beliefs of the parent mission churches. The next three were 'revivalist', deriving their inspiration from prophets and mediums. The last two were 'syncretist', openly or implicitly mingling Christian and African beliefs and practices.

Bethel and Eleja were linked to Anglican and Methodist parent Churches in Nigeria, but separated from them over the issue of polygamy. Plural marriage was a divisive matter throughout Africa, and there had long been debates about whether surplus wives should be sent away when their husbands became Christians, and whether polygamists could take Holy Communion or hold office in the church. Many polygamists had supported the churches in their beginnings, and claimed that, even if their marriage customs were different from those of Europeans, they had Christian faith. They possessed the Bible, often partly or wholly in their own language, and learned from it that the great patriarchs, not to mention King Solomon, had numerous wives. Even the New Testament, they pointed out, only required that bishops and deacons should be husbands of 'one wife', and said nothing of other church members (1 Timothy 3:2, 12).

In Porto Novo it had been a French Methodist missionary, Henri Arnett in 1900, who claimed that some of the leaders of Ouézoumé church were practising polygamy and put them 'under discipline', suspension or excommunication. This caused a great disturbance and a commission of inquiry, composed of ministers and lay leaders, went to the Methodist churches in Lagos to seek guidance and re-establish order, but no clear decision was reached. Arnett insisted on excluding polygamists from church membership, and the result was schism. The dissidents left and formed what was first called 'L'Église de l'Union Africaine' but later developed into two groups, Bethel and Eleja, their first church being opened in 1901.

Years later leaders of Eleja told me how their predecessors had annoyed Arnett by singing outside his windows at Ataké at night, 'We do not want to be, In your society.' That it was sung in English, to a French missionary, was even more irritating. But by 1936 passions had cooled, and these separated Methodists sought closer relations with their mother church. They still used the old translations of the Prayer Book and the Bible, had the same hymns and psalms, and claimed to follow orthodox doctrine. They said that the sole difference was over the ancient custom of plural marriages, which (they hinted) was still practised secretly by some members of modern Ouézoumé.

The popular name 'Eleja' was Yoruba, meaning 'fishmonger', and it came from Lagos where the first separating polygamous Methodists built their church next to the fish market. The name stuck and spread, and in Porto Novo the church was known as 'Le Temple des Marchands de Poissons (Eledja)'. The members were aware of the use of a fish symbol in early Christianity, and inside their Porto Novo church a symbolic copper fish was nailed on the pulpit.

For a time the Nigerian headquarters of Bethel (Anglican) and Eleja (Methodist) Churches provided ministers or leaders for the Porto Novo branches, but that was difficult because, to be fully useful, they needed to be French-speaking. One weakness of the Independents was the poor training of their clergy, compared with the Seminary-based preparation of the catechists and ministers in the official Church.

The Cherubim and Seraphim societies began in Nigeria, but spread to neighbouring countries, and later to Europe. In 1920, a prophet named Moses Tunolashe gathered a prayer group in Lagos and claimed to heal by faith. He was supported from 1925 by a young Anglican woman, Miss Abiodun, who saw angels in visions. Called 'Seraphim' at first, after the angelic visionary helpers, they were given through a further revelation the full name of 'Cherubim and Seraphim' as named in the Te Deum in the Anglican Prayer Book.

In Porto Novo 'Les Chérubins et Séraphins' were led by prophets and prophetesses, always wearing blue or white robes. It may be noted that followers of the ancient oracle Fa (Ifa) also wear blue or white robes. Similarly, as the devotees of Fa carry and wave rods, so Cherubim prophets may carry rods inscribed with the divine name 'Eloi' and wave them in the air during prayers. These societies did not use formal prayer books, and their local chorus hymns were more meaningful than the stilted translations used by mission churches.

The churches of Christianisme Céleste and Christique attracted some Protestants and a few Catholics. Crucifixes and candles figured in their worship. One of their prophets told me that, although he was very young, a divine voice had commanded him to wear white robes. His prophetical movement refused to use indigenous magical 'medicines', but anointed sick people with oil, following biblical injunctions. Holy water was also used, and ashes on Ash Wednesday and at other times of penitence.

The syncretistic Independents tried to make a deliberate fusion of Christian and indigenous religions. In Lagos a journalist had sought to identify Christianity with the Ifa oracle, called Orunmila, 'heaven knows salvation'. Divination was declared to have been practised in the Bible, in Joseph's cup and in the Urim and Thummim of the priests. An Ifa priest, they said, was following Christ, whom the epistle to the Hebrews declared was a priest after the order of the non-Israelite Melchizedek. The Porto Novo Orunmila community followed this attempt to join together Christianity and the Fa oracle, its version of the Yoruba Ifa (see Genesis 44:2; Exodus 28:30; Hebrews 7:17).

L'Église des Oracles was part of the same process. Its chapel was in traditional form but, instead of a cross or crucifix in the sanctuary, a tree bearing the nuts that were used in Fa divination was painted on the wall.

The walls in the nave had other pictures: the Fa divining board, cords of sacred nuts, and a chalice-like cup for the nuts. There were also designs of birds and snakes, such as could be seen on the walls of indigenous 'pagan' temples in the town. There was also a picture of a woman with large breasts, painted in the sacred colours, red, blue and white.

Although these were only small chapels, with few followers, they were growing in the 1930s, and Eleja, Cherubim and Seraphim, the African National Church, and the Church of the Lord (Aladura, prayer church) were soon to become much more powerful forces in the religious life of Nigeria, Dahomey, and other lands.

* * * * *

Islam was older in Porto Novo than Christianity, but in the 1930s it was not widespread in the southern parts of Dahomey. Particularly in the central region round Abomey, the traditional national religion was entrenched, with little presence of Christianity or Islam. In neighbouring Nigeria, there were many Muslims among the Yoruba, but few among the Igbo.

Islam was introduced to Porto Novo towards the end of the eighteenth century. King Dé Ayikpé gave the Muslims land and a mosque was built, its worship being led by an Imam from Ilorin in Nigeria. Five other mosques were soon erected in the town, and one was at Ataké, opposite our mission house. When we lived there for a short time, we would be wakened before dawn by the first call to prayer in Arabic. Soon the voices of Muslim children would be heard reciting, in singsong, verses from the Koran, though they did not understand Arabic apart from the formal prayers.

Porto Novo Muslims had a long period of peace under colonial rule, though they, like the Protestants, would probably have preferred British rule to French, because of their links with Nigeria. But the French government, with its large commitments to Muslim communities in North Africa, sought their co-operation and gave freedom of worship.

In 1913 there arose keen divisions in the Muslim community in Porto Novo over a project for construction of a great central mosque, next to the principal market in the centre of the old town. Tension between two parties became so acute that it almost led to civil war, and work on the mosque was suspended from 1914 to 1926.

The parties were led by people of different origins, one by Paraiso, descended from former Portuguese colonials, the other by Akindelé, of the Goun-Yoruba side. After long debates Akindelé met Paraiso one day coming home from Friday prayers and asked him to his house. He reminded Paraiso that formerly his father would kill a bull every Friday for his followers, organize dances and songs, and himself join in. Akindelé now asked the son, Paraiso, to follow his father's generosity. Paraiso agreed, a bull was killed, Paraiso and Akindelé danced, and the work on the great mosque was taken up and soon finished.

When we were in Porto Novo in the thirties the central mosque was in full use, as were several smaller mosques, and the community seemed to be at peace. Islam had always been favoured by the rulers of the town and had considerable influence in public affairs.

The central mosque was a large building, with an ornate front of concrete painted yellow. Inside it was plain, of course, with mats on the floor, and a high pulpit at the far end, with a grandfather clock nearby. The sole decoration was of verses from the Koran, in Arabic lettering, inscribed on the walls. Women swept the floors and did the cleaning, but they did not attend public prayers, making their devotions at home. The Ahmadiyya sect was active in West Africa, in the Gold Coast and Nigeria, but we did not meet it at that time in Porto Novo.

8. VOODOO

Although in the 1930s Christianity and Islam were well established in Porto Novo and had advantages through government and education, the majority of the inhabitants of the town and the country round about followed the traditional religion of their ancestors.

This religion may rightly be called 'Voodoo', because that West Indian word came from the language of Dahomey, where *vudu* or *vodoun* indicated a god or supernatural spirit. During the slave trade millions of people were transported from Africa to different parts of the Americas, and slaves from Dahomey, from wars of old Abomey, were taken particularly to Haiti. Haitian Voodoo came into being as a mixture of Dahomean *vodoun* and Roman Catholicism. But in Dahomey itself *vodoun* referred specifically to families of gods with their own temples, priests and devotees. (See chapter 3.)

Like most African peoples, the Goun of Porto Novo believed in a supreme deity, God. He was not a *vodoun* but was above them all. He had no temples or regular cultus, though it is said that in the ancient city of Abomey there was a cult of a superior *vodoun* named Mawu.

In the traditional religion of most of the country one title for the supreme deity was Mawu (or Maou), a name that was said to mean 'none greater'. This title was commonly used in ancient proverbs and legends, and it had been adopted by Roman Catholics as the equivalent of God. Yet in the old Capuchin *Doctrina Christiana* of 1660, God was translated 'Vodu' and Jesus was 'Lisa', another deity or consort.

In our time in Porto Novo the Protestant name for God was Djihwé-yehwé, a fairly simple compound word meaning 'sky-house-spirit'.

* * * * *

Porto Novo in the 1930s was a treasure house of religion, with countless wayside shrines and larger temples. As in the Bible, spirits were worshipped 'on every high hill and under every green tree', more or less. But it was easy to dismiss these sacred places as 'fetish' or 'paganism', or ignore them because they were rarely found in the official and shopping areas of the newer parts of the town, or were hidden away in family compounds.

The most common and evident wayside shrines in the old town were little thatched shelters covering simple mud pillars, conical in shape and often in human form, adorned with cowrie shells. A clay or wooden image might be rough or plain, often with female breasts, though it could be spoken of as 'he'. This figure was Legba (called Eshu by the Yoruba people) and was sometimes formerly called 'the devil' by foreigners. Legba (Eshu) was believed to be a protective spirit, admittedly of a dangerous or mischievous nature, but for that very reason useful as a guardian of houses, fields or villages.

There were very many little Legba shrines, though their numbers greatly declined with the coming of new roads and modern buildings. They were regarded as protectors of people and places. In the mornings householders would offer a few beans or grains of maize at these little shrines or, on special occasions, pour out libations of oil and blood.

A phallic element was strong in the cult of Legba, and he was invoked to give fertility. A rough wooden phallus was often stuck at the foot of the main image, and small mounds next to it might represent his wives and children. All of them received offerings in small dishes or libations in little umbrella-like metal standards (asen).

In 1936, on the Adjarra roadside out of Porto Novo, there appeared a new and striking clay Legba. It took the form of a life-size naked man, painted red like a European, wearing only a sun helmet and a wristwatch, and with a large wooden phallus. Covered by a thatched roof, it stood to protect a group of houses surrounded by fields of maize and cassava. This and other Legbas were the first and most obvious signs of 'heathenism' to strike the new arrival in Dahomey.

* * * * *

The next activity to force itself on attention in Porto Novo at that time was the secret society called Zangbeto, 'hunters of the night', also named 'spirits of the sea'.

The noises of the Zangbeto society during the night disturbed people in the older parts of the town. One missionary shot or threatened to shoot at them, and another, having thrown a bowl of water over them as they passed, shouting, beneath his window, failed to diminish their noise.

The Zangbeto is said to have been introduced to Porto Novo by the founder of the town, Té Agbanlin, who ruled from 1688. The society was encouraged by the kings, and tolerated by the later French government, because it claimed to chase away thieves, though it operated in the older parts of the town and not among modern administrative buildings.

From about eight o'clock in the evening, when it was always dark, the sounds of hollow horns were heard in old quarters of Porto Novo. This was a signal for all women to take their children indoors, and not to look out again. When the roads were deserted and fires put out, the members of the society gathered together. One of them, dressed in a long grass robe and crowned with horns or a mask with two holes to see through, represented the spirit of Zangbeto. It was strictly forbidden, however, to suggest that the robes were occupied by men, and even Muslims and Christians might be in trouble if they said so openly. The robes and masks of the Zangbeto could sometimes be seen in the daytime, hanging under small thatched shelters in older parts of the town, and it was taboo to touch them.

The Zangbeto and their assistants, *zan-si,* 'wives of the night', ran through the streets, blowing horns, banging gongs and shaking rattles. They shouted out in nasal tones, in the way that spirits and the departed were believed to speak. At times they met in groves in the bush, to admit new candidates, who were questioned on their beliefs in Zangbeto, beaten in trials of endurance, and charged to bring offerings as fees of membership.

Another society, Bligédé, came from Yoruba country to Porto Novo in 1920, and also acted as night-watchmen. They did not wear the costumes or have the mythology of the Zangbeto, but they also banged gongs and patrolled the streets of the eastern quarters of the town by night.

With these societies, and regular policemen, it might be thought that theft and burglary would disappear. But since the Zangbeto and others made so much noise and, as well as keeping the roads clear, spent time on their own rituals, it was not hard for determined thieves to operate in quieter places or after the societies' members had moved on.

It must be said that in twenty years in Africa we never had any burglaries, or lost any money or property from our houses. In villages we slept with doors and windows open, and left them unlocked if we walked away. One exception, involving theft from a car by a foreign employee at Dassa, will be mentioned later.

* * * * *

The Zangbeto and similar masked groups were concerned with the dead and belief in survival, but there were many other expressions of faith in the *vodouns*, the gods. In and beyond Porto Novo there were sacred thickets or spinneys, often round a giant iroko tree (African oak) or a squat baobab tree. At its foot, or in the middle of a field, there were mounds of earth, small wooden or clay statues, and a clay altar behind a curtain of white cloth. The figures represented the *vodouns*, the divinities and their attendants worshipped at that place.

There were small temples in the old town and some larger ones outside. In the 1930s a large new temple appeared on the Adjarra road. The first building was as big as a house, and its carefully moulded earthen walls were decorated with geometrical designs. But this was only the vestibule, and beyond it, in a courtyard and sheltered by a tall tree, stood the principal building, in which were clay and wooden figures of divinities and altars for offerings.

One of the most significant gods of old Porto Novo was the serpent Dan or Dangbé, the non-poisonous python. The cult of the python is found along the Dahomean seaboard, with its lagoons and rivers. Tradition said that the founder of Porto Novo, having difficulties in warfare, was advised to seek the protection of Dangbé. A couple of pythons were brought in a sack and installed in a round hut in the royal compound. The pythons would come out of the hut at the priest's call, and receive food and worship, and prayers

67

from devout visitors. Pythons were strictly taboo, never killed, and saluted by kissing the ground and calling them 'father', since they were regarded as ancestors. If a python was found in our seminary garden, as happened at times, it would be lifted up carefully on a rake, and put over the wall for somebody else to reverence.

Other Dangbé temples were established in Porto Novo, and the chief priest was given a special area of the town which he called after his own village, Ouézoumé. In one part of this quarter, as we have seen, the Methodist church was later built.

Further popular divinities were the storm god So or Hevioso (Yoruba Shango), the smallpox deity Sakpata (Shokpona), and the god of iron and warfare Gu (Ogun). There were royal divinities, with images inside and outside the palace of the King of the Night – about whom, more below – having special attendants. There were official gods and personal ones, some of which were introduced, because of their supposed protective ability, from other places.

A god Ata was brought to the town from a distant village and installed in a quarter named after it, Ata-Ké, near the mission house in the northern part of the town but within its walls. Ata's worship took place every five days, the day of the great market of Porto Novo.

Both a god in his own right and messenger to other gods was Fa (Yoruba Ifa). This was an oracle consulted on many occasions in religious and social life and, like Legba, it could be attached to any of the other gods. The Fa was said to have come from Yoruba country, and perhaps it originated even farther off, since it involved a system of marking which resembled writing otherwise unknown in these regions. Fa was a system of divination or fortune-telling, operated by a diviner called Bokonon (Yoruba Babalawo), 'father of mysteries'. It involved complicated systems of geomancy or earth-divination, by which the wills of the gods were sought, fortunes told or messages transmitted.

* * * * *

In old Porto Novo, and in the suburbs and villages beyond, there could be seen what were popularly known as 'convents', in Goungbé *houn-kpamé*, 'spirit's enclosure'. These were collections of mud huts, surrounded by a mud or concrete wall and marked by a white flag.

Here the training of priests and their acolytes took place, in remarkable detail, and with the aim of bringing about a complete change of personality, by simulated death and resurrection. In 1945 I obtained from a friend of mine, Honvo, details of this system of training which otherwise was hidden from the laity and especially from foreigners.

A priest was called *Vodoun-on* or *Houn-on*, 'owner of the god', and each active assistant or acolyte was a *vodoun-si*, 'wife of the god'. This did not imply any sexual rituals, as some have supposed, but it did indicate the close relationship of the devotee to the deity. Priests were usually selected by a hereditary system, a priestly family choosing the most suitable of its members for the office. Devotees *(vodoun-si)* were picked from families that worshipped the particular deity. In the past both male and female 'wives of the god' were chosen, but under French colonial rule many young men were conscripted for military service, especially before and during World War II. Vodoun-sis, then, were chiefly women, though there were some men if they could find substitutes to go into the army.

Recruitment for the convents took place at different times of the year, according to the god worshipped, and normally it coincided with the annual ceremony for the coming out of trained devotees. Public dances were arranged for nine days, with drumming, and some dancers fell into trances. Those who had been selected by the god, in consultation with the oracle Fa, took part in the dances and often were possessed, with loud cries and convulsions. This was regarded as a mark of favour and choice by the deity. Those who were in states of trance were taken into the convent and laid before the image or altar of the divinity. Their hair was shaved off, and a bath given of water from a special river. Hair and nail clippings were kept as charms against infidelity. All clothes were taken away, and devotees were given simple skirts or loincloths.

My friend Honvo refused to accept his selection, which had been decided by his father and a priest, so he was seized by night and bundled into the convent. Then he was given training with other devotees, learning songs and dances and doing household duties.

The aim of the training of priests and acolytes was that they would become new personalities, distinct from ordinary people. It was a process of dying to the old life and rising to a new, since in trances they were often carried as if dead into the convent and wrapped in shrouds, and when they regained consciousness they seemed to be different beings. There were special foods, allowed or taboo, dances, prayers and offerings.

Devotees were marked with characteristic tattoos on the face and body, and the scars often went septic and had to be washed with medicines. In particular, there was a special language or dialect of each cult to be learnt. For example, followers of So or Shango, the thunder god, which was of Yoruba origin, were taught Yoruba words and formulas.

After six to nine months the devotees were ready to leave the convent at a great festival or dance. After another head shaving and a ritual bath, they would be dressed in rich costumes and showed obvious tattoos. They danced all day and visited important temples in the neighbourhood. With new names, costumes and dialects they returned to their families, but at first would hardly be able to understand their own language. Only little by little did they learn their mother tongue and fit into family life.

Married or engaged women had been chaste during all their time in the convent, and they had to get permission from the Fa oracle to return to their homes and husbands. Women had to sit in turn on a mat, with legs stretched out, and a small boy of six to eight years of age sat on their laps to make formal renewal with the opposite sex. Then the females could take up family life again, but they were still 'wives of the god', and they would go back to the convent at great festivals and join in the dances which might entail further trances.

Honvo followed this ritual perforce but, after his return to family life, he only took part half-heartedly in temple prayers, and finally abandoned them altogether. His companions threatened to beat him, and on his mother's advice Honvo left his village and travelled miles on foot till he reached the coastal town of Cotonou. He stayed there and got work, was attracted to the church community and was baptized as André. Only years later was he able to return home.

* * * * *

Controlling the gods and secret societies in Porto Novo was the 'King of the Night', a title used even by republican French administrators. The formal 'King of the Day', recognized head of the people of the town, was successor of the founders of Porto Novo.

But the 'King of the Night', or more properly the Zoun-on, 'Master of the Forest', represented the original owners of the land, who were said to have come from Ijebu in southern Nigeria. He was called the Father of the King, and it was at his palace that the Fa oracle was consulted to know whether a new Day King was worthy of reigning. He was also responsible for a symbolic washing of the king before his installation.

After the coronation the two kings might never meet, and to make sure that this taboo was observed, the one only went out of his palace during the daytime, and the other only at night. The King of the Night must never venture out during the day, or see the King of the Day.

This strong taboo was threatened in 1942 when the French authorities commanded the King of the Night to go to the police station during the daytime, under suspicion of contacts with 'enemy' Nigeria. Rather than commit this fatal breach, the King of the Night stayed in his palace, took poison, and died. This calamity and the death in prison at Dakar of Pastor Ernest Taylor, which we will recount later, shook Porto Novo town and neighbourhood.

9. LES DEMOISELLES

During the 1930s and '40s, when most male teachers and ministers had returned to Britain and France, continuity in the European staff of the Methodist church and mission in Porto Novo was provided by two French ladies.

Suzanne Escande was short with fair wavy hair, rather prim but with a sense of humour. She came from a Reformed church community in Paris. Suzanne Marlier was also short, darker and slim, but more open and with twinkling eyes. She was a Lutheran from Alsace. The two were always called Les Demoiselles, or The Demoiselles, a term that was also used to refer to the whole girls' school in Porto Novo, which they directed and typified.

Missionaries in India and China would serve for a period, a 'tour', of five to seven years before returning to Europe on leave or 'furlough'. But in West Africa, whose climate had proved so deadly, eighteen months was the normal tour, followed by up to six months in Europe. The two Demoiselles, however, were an exception. Their joint work was so vital to the girls' school that, having stayed in Dahomey for the school terms, they went on leave every year, spending two or three summer months in France during the long vacation. (We followed the same pattern in the fifties when working at the university college in Nigeria.)

When the war came, with German occupation of much of France, it was impossible for these Demoiselles to get home to Paris or Alsace. So they stayed in Porto Novo throughout the six years of the war, enduring the climate but getting tired and weak. After the war they retired to France, hoping that the African teachers they had trained would be able to carry on, despite the lack of outside help.

At first the Demoiselles conducted the girls' school in the Ataké mission house. But the ground floor rooms were small, dark and quite inadequate and, soon after their arrival, plans were made for a new school. The new premises, constructed just beyond the Seminary and near open land on the Boulevard which partly encircled northern Porto Novo, were opened about 1936.

The fine concrete building was a large square, with classrooms, offices and kitchens on the ground floor, teachers' rooms on the upper floor of one wing and girls' dormitories along another. Here the Demoiselles realized their dream of having a largely boarding school, where everyone from a distance – and girls came from all over the country – could be housed and a number of day girls could also be entered though there were some pupils, local girls from Porto Novo town and others staying with relatives, who lived out, the Demoiselles wished to have as many as possible under their direct care, to form both their education and their character. For this they were highly respected by Dahomean parents.

* * * * *

Every Sunday morning a procession of girls from the school set out to walk down through the town at eight thirty, to attend morning service at Ouézoumé church. It was later but as regular as attendance at school on weekdays, and few absences were permitted. If, for example, a girl wanted to be away at a family gathering at the weekend, she had to get written permission from the headmistress, Suzanne Escande.

Most of the girls were from Protestant families in various parts of Dahomey and Togo, but a few were Catholics and others of no particular religion but with parents who wanted them to get a sound French education. There were Catholic and state schools for girls as well, with limited accommodation, but the Demoiselles had a high reputation, which made their school popular, and there was always a waiting list.

In white Sunday dresses and yellow-blue headscarves, the girls marched two by two through the town. While at that time many Dahomeans, especially girls and women, went barefoot at home and for daily work, the schoolgirls wore shoes or sandals, which were often slipped off in class, or even in church, and put on again hurriedly if spotted by teachers.

Two African teachers went in front of the girls' procession and two behind, with the European Demoiselles bringing up in the rear, Escande often carrying a parasol. When the school was at Ataké, the Dahomean teachers lived in Porto Novo town. The married ones had to find rooms for themselves and their children, and domestic responsibilities often made getting to school on time difficult, though punctuality was required. Single women were open to other problems. Sometimes they were young ladies who, being proud of their education, tried to dress like Paris fashion models, with the result that some people doubted their morality. The Demoiselles would deny any impropriety but rigorously investigate any hint of it. They were trying to train their best pupils as teachers and had taken one or two into their home. Marie Gaba, daughter of a Methodist minister from Togo, was especially promising.

Down the narrow lanes of the town the crocodile procession made its way between houses and past shops. The girls walked at a slow and rhythmical pace, attracting the scrutiny of people in houses, open-sided shelters and workplaces. Women watched them, some with pride or concern if their own children were in the company. Others looked critically at the girls in foreign clothes, or envied their dresses and well-fed appearance.

Old and young men observed the light and dark faces, comely figures, swaying hips, shapely legs and ankles. Under the girls' bandannas could be discerned hair styles in long plaits tied up in buns, or squares pulled tightly in knots, the products of Saturday afternoon hairdressing.

In the forties, students from the Seminary and older boys from the new Methodist boys' school did not march to church in order, but they were expected to be there. They found ways of following the procession of girls or coming upon it at street corners, where they saw the girls face to face and looked for some who were specially favoured. With teachers at front and back the girls were well guarded, but it was impossible to prevent glances going from boys to girls and back, and hard to stop the passing of notes in the crowds or in church.

Moreover, notes could be passed, but with more difficulty, at the five o'clock evening service in the seminary chapel – always conducted in French and therefore specially important – which the girls also attended.

Suzanne Escande kept a sharp look out for any males who met the procession of girls by design or apparent chance. She was a strict disciplinarian and had built up the reputation of the girls' school as a place of learning and virtue, for which she was trusted by parents. The girls seemed to be models of propriety, but the fires of adolescence that burned within them could be suspected or noticed in small acts or looks.

Suzanne Marlier was more easygoing and looked kindly on the senior young men, if she knew them to be serious and of good family. She had five brothers at home in Alsace, and was used to family life and male company. Her warm nature gave her sympathy with girls and youths and, while they accepted the discipline of the headmistress, it was to Mademoiselle Marlier that girls often turned with hopes or troubles. She would not pass on any notes that were intercepted, but she did not always show them to Escande and destroyed them quietly after noting the names on both sides. She helped fix marriages by pressing parents to accept a girl's choice, if at all possible, instead of making arrangements between families first.

It was the custom in Dahomey, as in other countries, for parents to propose marriage without asking the children involved, sometimes arranging an alliance with another family even before the children were born. But in the thirties young people were beginning to assert their own wishes, and the educated spoke of 'love'. Schools could be outposts of the new ways, and were often accused of breaking down the old morality. But the Porto Novo Protestant Girls' School was both an agent of marriages by choice and a guardian of the chastity of its pupils.

* * * * *

It was an unwritten rule for the newest missionary both to carve the turkey at the mission Christmas dinner and to play the part of Père Noël (Father Christmas) at the girls' school.

Africa had been introduced to the Victorian custom of a Christmas tree – a local casuarina tree which resembled a fir – together with the charade of a robed Santa Claus or Saint Nicholas, whose feast fell, near the end of term, on 6th December.

So in December 1933 I went nervously to endure my initiation in the largest room of the girls' school, which was then still at Ataké. Bare electric lights hung from the ceiling and, although it was dark outside, the room was crowded and very hot. Teachers and parents sat on two sides of the room, and girls on the others, leaving some space in the centre. There were friends and relatives from the town, and it was surprising to see a French woman suckling a baby. This was a common sight among African women, but more rare with whites.

There were carols, recitations and short plays at first, and then Mlle Marlier took me out quietly to another classroom where the Father Christmas costume was laid out. This had red top and bottom pieces and even a white beard, which was very hot. I put these on, took up a sack of presents, and went back into the classroom. There was great excitement and, with Marlier's help, the gifts, which had been carefully prepared by the teachers, were distributed to each girl.

Some children were surprised and even fearful at the Père Noël figure, but one sharp little girl was heard remarking, 'That man has the same shoes on as the other man who sat over there,' pointing to my former chair.

I had only kept on vest and pants underneath the costume and, when I went into the side room to change back, they were soaked with sweat and partly stained with red.

* * * * *

In 1945 I was having dinner with the Demoiselles at the girls' school when news came through of the overwhelming Labour victory in Britain in the general election. There was an English teacher present who had come from the Ivory Coast to help in the changeover from the Demoiselles, who were preparing for their long delayed leave and retirement in France. She was shocked by the election result and said, 'It's those young soldiers. They don't know how to vote.'

But Mlle Marlier winked at me, and I retorted, 'They know how to die for their country.'

Marlier's brothers in Alsace had all suffered in the war and one, a pastor, had been sent to a concentration camp, where he contracted tuberculosis and barely survived.

Shortly afterwards, a newspaper arrived with a picture of Prime Minister Clement Attlee with King George VI, and Marlier exclaimed, 'Oh, il est brave' (he is nice, or gallant).

10. FIRST HOME

The old mission house in the Ataké quarter of Porto Novo was just within the old town walls but at a suitable distance from the centre and the lagoon. It was a large two-storey building, made of mud bricks covered with cement and whitewashed, and with a corrugated iron roof.

Downstairs there was an office and several class-rooms, used by the girls' school before their new school was built. At the back of the house, an outside wooden staircase led to the first floor quarters. There was a large lounge-dining-room, with fine mahogany floor boards which were kept polished. Verandas ran back and front to two bedrooms, a bathroom and a tiny pantry. There being no running water, bath water was carried up in cans by the houseboy, and 'night soil' was removed by the compound 'guardian' from the back veranda.

This was our first married home in October 1936, and we tried to settle in, to learn about housekeeping, to enter into church life, to know the church members and to discover the attractions of the town and shops. For the four months that we lived at Ataké before transferring to the seminary, the sole mission car was under our control, and it was lent to the different mission houses and schools for shopping expeditions.

Most of the stores were down near the lagoon, and there were shops of French, Swiss, British, Lebanese and Greek. The British shops were John Holt's and UAC (United Africa Company of Lever Brothers); the French CFAO (Compagnie Française de l'Afrique Occidentale) and Maison Druot; the Swiss, SCOA (Socété Commerciale de l'Ouest Africain); and the Greek, PZ (Paterson Zochonis). Other firms came in, and there were many smaller but often useful African stores. But we learned to bandy about these initials, confusing though they sometimes were.

These shops stocked foods likely to appeal to Europeans and increasing numbers of Africans as they took to European foods. Since at that time neither milk nor butter was available fresh in Porto Novo, we bought them in tins and kept them with other perishable goods in simple wire cages or thermos flasks. Meat, vegetables and fruit were purchased from wayside stalls or the main market, and usually the bargaining was left to the house cook.

We had a cook, as all our colleagues did, but it took time to get used to what his limited knowledge provided. Mary was not accustomed to French salad dressing and decided to make some mayonnaise from an English recipe. This came out well, but then there was a problem finding a glass jar or bottle. After searching vainly we cleaned out a jar of bath salts and used that, but no amount of boiling would completely disperse the perfume.

'Have some bath salts on your green salad,' we told a dinner guest. 'Quite a new taste.'

More serious was making cakes, beginning with simple scones. The small pantry was upstairs, but the kitchen was a hut downstairs and across the garden, where the Dahomean cook held sway. Having made some fine scones, from the best tinned butter since margarine was not available, Mary took them down the stairs and across the yard to the kitchen, where the cook eyed them suspiciously. She made signs to him to put the scones in the black range oven and pile more wood on the fire.

'Make it hot, but don't open the door,' she shouted. But her French was elementary and his English non-existent.

I was in the downstairs office when she came in, streaming with sweat in her light dress and red-faced under her sun helmet. She threw a tray of scones on the floor and cried, 'There are the scones. That cook has kept opening the oven door and they're as hard as nails.'

'They bounced,' I agreed. 'I don't know what the young husband should do. Find a rhino whip to beat the cook, or my wife, or pray for you. I expect we shall eat them when they get soft.'

We picked up the scones and dusted them, and they were quite good after a few days.

* * * * *

For a few months, I had the supervision of villages far beyond Porto Novo, and a call came from the Agegés, villages on the lagoon towards the port of Cotonou. We decided to pay a visit and to spend two nights there, since the journey would take several hours. Having packed a case and two camp beds, we set out, accompanied by a houseboy and the catechist who had come to guide us.

A dugout canoe was waiting at a small wharf and we were rowed towards the west in the early afternoon. The lagoon widened, and land on both sides was low-lying. It was very hot and humid, with very little breeze, and the calm, muddy water reflected the sun's rays, so that, when the first Agegé, a fishing village with all its houses built on piles in the water, came into view, it shimmered in the heat. We landed on a rickety stage near a little chapel, where we met church members, who gave us drinks and then sat around for talks and an early evening service. The catechist explained his problems: small numbers but new possibilities, realized in the event by the many churches and by the government tourist centres and night clubs established in that area.

After a light meal we went to bed, and then discovered one of the hardships of lagoon life. The small hut where we were to sleep was clean but full of mosquitoes. Our camp beds were set up and mosquito nets fitted, but the insects were so numerous that they got inside the nets and, although we caught many of them, there were others left.

Next day was hotter, there seemed to be even more mosquitoes, and there was another restless night. When we set off for the return journey after breakfast, the morning was still and stifling. Mary was flushed and developed a splitting headache, and the two-hour journey seemed endless. Although we were met by the chauffeur with the car at Porto Novo, every bump in the road seemed to go through her head.

At Ataké she went to bed at once and had malarial fever for two weeks. Aspirin was tried at first, and then the doctor from the hospital supplied stronger doses of quinine. Mary's mouth developed sores, which were treated with gentian violet and this marked her face and the bed sheets.

Television, of course, did not exist and we had no wireless or daily newspaper. We knew nothing of happenings in the outside world. One day in December, having cycled down to the central post office, I saw some surprising news on a telegraph sheet, so that I looked up several earlier numbers. Back home I asked Mary, 'Who is the King of England?'

'Edward the Eighth,' she replied.

'Wrong. It is George the Sixth.'

So we learned of the abdication and only later received the *Manchester Guardian Weekly* by sea mail and caught up with the events in detail.

* * * * *

After Synod in January 1937 we were moved from Ataké to the seminary and lived for four years in the principal's house. We inherited the faithful house 'boy' (man) Joseph and told him the news of the appointment.

'Directeur?' he asked, almost breathlessly, and was relieved on being reassured, as it affected his status.

Joseph was about thirty then, older than me, and had been trained by our predecessors, the Bishops, in English ways. He even knew how to show the cook the mysteries of making Yorkshire puddings, 'le pouding Yorkshire'. He was a married man, with a house in the middle of town, and sometimes brought his wife and children to see us. I found that he knew old Porto Novo traditions and would recount with awe some of the tales and songs of royal processions for the Porto Novo 'King of the Night'.

Every Sunday evening there was a service in French in the seminary chapel. It was the only regular French Protestant service in the town and some visitors came to it. Girls and boys from the schools and our seminary students formed most of the large congregation.

Of the visitors we soon got to know Hélène and Jacques Viéville. He worked in the government treasury and was a French Protestant, while she was a Roman Catholic.

'We were very well married,' she told us. 'First of all at the town hall, the mayor's office, as is obligatory, you know, in France. Then there was a

80

blessing in my own Catholic church and another one at Jacques' Protestant temple. We agreed that if we have children, the boys will follow their father's religion and the girls the mother's.' (As far as I know, they only had a son, who was at school in France at that time.) She continued, 'Jacques goes with me to the Latin mass at the Catholic cathedral here, but your Protestant church only has native language services in the evening, so we will come to your seminary French service, if you allow it.'

We were delighted and found a new outlet for Mary. Hélène, who spoke some English, was interested at once since Mary was a nurse.

'You should get a bicycle, then you could come and help at the Red Cross,' she said. 'Stir your husband up, I expect he's got a bike.'

'Well, everything here seems to be communal,' said Mary. 'There's one car between us all, and Mr Fairhurst is now at Ataké and has charge of it. Our furniture belongs to the seminary, even to the beds and sheets. My husband uses a college bicycle sometimes, but it's a man's. I expect the girls' school has one for women.'

'Then borrow that. Tell them you must break out of this closed atmosphere. It's almost like a convent.'

This was done and guided by Hélène Mary found her way through the narrow winding streets of Porto Novo to a group of Red Cross huts down by the lagoon. They were wooden and small, crowded with Dahomean women and their babies. A voluntary staff of nuns and wives of officials took it in turns to give a day or two each week to dispense simple medicines and examine serious cases before they were sent to the military hospital or the larger institution at Cotonou.

When she first arrived, Mary found that the French custom was to shake hands with everybody, that is all Europeans, and this was such a strain that she soon arranged to get there early and avoid making the round of helpers. Her French improved slowly, though she picked up some pidgin French, petit nègre, and military slang which had some surprises.

Back home she had difficulties with a new cook, Anani, trying to make him clean out his kitchen, which had cobwebs above the range and work bench. So she turned his table and chairs out into the garden, cleaning and whitewashing the place herself. Anani's pride was hurt. He insisted on putting things back himself, and then came to report his mistress to me.

'Femme là, il 'sulté moi,' he said in his mixed French. 'Il fou-camp moi.'

'Fou-camp', or 'Fous-moi le camp', was a coarse but common expression meaning 'Do a bunk', 'get out', 'scram', or worse.

'What did you say to Anani?' I asked.

'I told him to go home for the day,' she replied. 'I could do my own cooking, if it were not so hot.'

At the Red Cross Hélène apologised to Mary for forceful language.

'I'm afraid we do use basic words,' she admitted. 'The medical orderlies talk like that, and you may hear even the nuns use occasional direct terms. They say what people understand. It's no use employing the polite words of the Académie Française if you want black patients to understand. Many of these women have picked up their few words of French from the military, and you know that soldiers do not use the most proper language. Now, we've done enough for today. Come home with me and have a drink, it will break your journey.'

They pushed their bicycles up a little slope to where the bungalow overlooked the lagoon and faced towards a haze on distant coconut palms which hinted at the sea beyond. It always seemed cooler here and not so depressing as Porto Novo town behind them, and the thought of sea suggested openness and home.

'What will you have?' asked Hélène.

'Squash, please.'

'You mustn't always drink that orange stuff. It's too acid. Let me give you something better, with ice.'

She poured out a peppermint liqueur, and Mary was so thirsty that she drank it at a gulp.

'Steady on,' said Hélène. 'You should sip it. Let me fill it up again.'

Mary soon felt better, cool and relaxed. But when she stood up to go she came over faint.

'I can hardly feel my legs,' she complained.

'Oh dear, what will Jacques say? I'm doping his Protestants? You had better lie down till it passes off.'

'No, I must go home, and make sure lunch is prepared. It's late already.'

Mary mounted her bicycle and rode slowly through the Porto Novo streets, shaking but concentrating. When she got back to the seminary I was waiting outside, wondering if there had been an accident. When she saw me, she wobbled, caught her foot and fell off the bike.

I helped her up and smelt her breath.

'Drunken homecoming of missionary's wife,' I said. 'Mind your language.'

11. MASTERY OF SEX

'When you come out to Dahomey, will you please bring me a book I have seen advertised? It is published in England and called *The Mastery of Sex,* by Leslie Weatherhead. I will pay you for it when you arrive.'

I had received this request from Paul Hoffer before we left home in 1936 and took the book with me. Hoffer had read a review of it, and perhaps the title 'Mastery' appealed to his dominating nature. I found that he had other works on the physiology of sex, and no doubt he wanted to look at the Christian viewpoints of this book.

'I hope this is what you needed,' I said, handing the book to him in Porto Novo.

'Ah, yes. Thank you. Have you read it?'

'Quite instructive.'

Leslie Weatherhead was a popular Methodist minister and psychologist, and his book gave frank accounts, unusual in those days, of sexual relationships, descriptions of male and female anatomy, and references to other books on birth control. It had caused a stir and was condemned by our College Governor. Some wag put a new cover on it to make it look like a thriller with the title and author, *The Mystery of Six* by Wesley Featherbed, and so it circulated among the students in secret.

In the 1930s, and in religious environments, sex was a taboo subject, but there were many problems. At our college there were seventy young men, mostly in their twenties, all celibates and forbidden by the rules of the church to marry during the period from acceptance for ministerial training until ordination seven years later. Then, it seemed to be assumed, all would get married and abandon celibacy. The regulations were strict, and no concessions were made to the feelings of individuals or the needs of special circumstances. That it might have been better for a man to have a companion in lonely situations, in Britain or overseas, was not allowed to alter traditional legislation. Seven years must be served, as Jacob did for Leah or Rachel.

I had become engaged, my fiancée and I were very much in love, and after four years of my training, in 1933, I asked the Mission House for permission to get married before going to Africa. This was refused, as the rule indicated that I must wait till the Conference of July 1936. When I replied that perhaps then I should not go overseas yet, that was accepted and I was told to enter the home work. As I was determined to go abroad, I had to submit and go alone.

I went to Dahomey in 1933 and was due for leave in eighteen months. But that would be in 1935 and would have involved returning to Africa still single and postponing marriage, if it was to be among family and friends, until the next leave in 1937. So I prolonged my first stay in Africa and remained till January 1936, to the sadness and strain of my fiancée and myself. Even on return to England, being young and unknown and from a remote French-speaking district, I had little work to do, and few deputation appointments. I asked for permission to marry only a month or two early, and not wait for the regulation July. But that again was refused.

It is said that one well known man got married just two weeks before his seven years was up. He was rebuked publicly by the President of the Conference, and replied, 'I am sorry, Mr President. I assure you it will not happen again.'

He was lucky to have only a public reprimand. Others who broke the rules had been given a year or two of extra probation, married but on a single man's salary, or dismissed the service.

After the Second World War all that changed. Leaders and their followers had come to broader and more charitable views. Married men, often with children, were admitted to ministerial training, and restrictions were virtually abolished. Some of us who had borne the burden and the heat of the day thought the relaxation went too far, and men should remain single, or engaged, until they had finished their college studies. Then women were admitted to the ministry, though not till the 1970s, a change that we had hardly ever considered.

Weatherhead's book was studied and discussed in college. For one of our students, aged twenty-two, it was a shocking revelation. He had no knowledge of the facts of sexual intercourse, and he could hardly believe that his parents and people he knew could have practised it. Most of us had some ideas but now learnt fuller details.

Although few were engaged or had 'understandings' when they entered college, it seemed to be assumed that we would find young ladies, often on Sunday or weekend visits to churches or missions round London or other training places. College parties were held to which our girl friends were openly invited. Marriage, after seven years, was regarded as the proper goal for ministers at home and overseas. Evangelical Anglican colleges, as well as Free Church, encouraged their student clergy to get married immediately their training was over. There was no idealization of celibacy for life, as in Anglo-Catholic circles or Roman Catholic discipline.

Weatherhead approved of birth control, and indicated where contraceptives could be bought, by post, under plain covers. But he advised engaged couples not to practise intercourse with contraceptives, because of the risks of accidents and the strains which the fear of unwanted pregnancy could produce, and he gave examples from his own psychiatric practice of sexual tragedies. The ideal was chastity, and sexual intercourse was the seal of marriage.

In the main we followed his advice, practising contraception later, only within marriage, to help space the family. AIDS was of course unknown, and modern advertisements and shop displays of condoms would have shocked us. They were called French Letters then, or contraceptives.

Nearly all our seventy students married eventually, and I know of only one who remained a bachelor all his life, living with his sisters. Homosexuality was rarely mentioned, or understood. Radclyffe Hall's book, *The Well of Loneliness,* had appeared in 1928, was condemned shrilly by some newspapers and eventually was banned for obscenity. But we hardly knew what it was concerned with and, reading it many years later, it seemed very mild. *Lady Chatterley's Lover* was not obtainable in full in England until 1960, but there were foreign editions. A copy of one of them was on the open shelves of our university library in Ibadan in 1950 and did not seem to interest African students.

In theological colleges there was a fairly free and inquiring atmosphere among students religious and sexual matters, and many became engaged, keeping to the seven year rule. I rarely heard of men having problems, but these could appear later when they went out into the world.

One student mentioned that he was accosted by prostitutes in London. But he was a Welsh poet, a dreamer, who strolled slowly through Leicester Square or over Waterloo Bridge, where girls spoke to him. Our advice was to walk quickly, as if he had some important business or appointment, and this seemed to work.

* * * * *

Single men, or married, might encounter temptation after leaving the seclusion of college for the diversity of life in English cities or lands overseas.

Africa came as a lively and uninhibited experience. In the 1930s much more than today, African women in towns and villages were often bare to the waist, understandably in such a hot and humid climate. Even in church women suckled their babies, made easy with a traditional two-piece costume. To a European, especially of church upbringing, such sights could be disturbing until he got used to them, if he ever did.

Men were often stripped for work, and in the far north of Dahomey, among the Somba people whom I visited later, men could be seen regularly wearing no clothes except thin stiff penis-sheaths, which bobbed up and down as they walked. Somba women wore only bunches of leaves and no more, even in the small Roman Catholic churches.

In the thirties Europeans, and ourselves and colleagues after the seven year period of celibacy, often took their wives with them to Africa. But, as was said earlier, the British thought that white children could not survive the tropics, and this caused many stresses, with wives staying in Britain or leaving their children behind for months.

Outside the missions it was rumoured that most, if not all, white men who had no European wife with them, would take an African mistress, or more. It is impossible to verify such a claim but one of my friends, an administrator, took his African partner with him on our travels, and they had two coffee-coloured children. In the schools, Catholic and Protestant, there were usually some coloured or half-caste girls and boys.

Sexual tensions appeared among us in different ways. A teacher colleague came to stay with us from the west. We saw that he had a fever and put him to bed, but he held on to both of us and insisted on talking.

'It is more than malaria,' he said. 'I get it from time to time. It is the loneliness – and temptation. You are married and don't know how it is. I am an active person and can't stand being alone. Last week the two other teachers had gone and I was clearing up from the end of term. Perhaps there was some fever, but there was also desire. I was confused and intoxicated. I felt I must have a woman. It seems that I called my boy Marc in the night and told him to fetch a girl from the village. I had heard that there were loose people, even in such a small place. Marc says he was frightened and refused at first, until I threatened to beat him. Then he was scared and called one.'

'He brought you a woman? To the school?'

'Yes. But it was no use. That's the folly and tragedy of it. I could not do anything. My mind must have been so divided, or I was too drunk, and in my shame I sent her away.'

'What did Marc think? Or the woman?'

'You need not worry. I doubt if she was an innocent.'

'But the scandal?'

'Nobody will know anything about it. Marc is a stranger from beyond the Gold Coast.'

'Is he trustworthy? As for keeping it quiet, everybody knows what white men do here.'

'That's why I feel so ashamed.'

'Well, you were impotent, so let's hope nothing more will come of it.'

'But there's Agnes.'

'You're not engaged to her?'

'No, I would like to be. I have not dared to ask her, and I cannot after this.'

'Not necessarily. But she's gone on furlough, and you had better ask for sick leave too.'

'What about the school?'

'It will have to manage. It usually does. There are monitors who can be given a chance.'

So it happened. He went on compassionate leave for health reasons. The following year he was married, though how much he told his wife is anybody's guess.

* * * * *

Like Victorian households, colonial establishments in Africa included numerous servants. Government and trading officials might have up to a dozen retainers, and even the missions could not dispense with small numbers.

In Porto Novo we tried to cut down servants to a basic cook and 'steward', a general houseboy. But there might appear a cook's 'small boy', a washerman for heavy items, a communal gardener, porter and nightwatchman. We were employers, and if we did not take in servants we might be regarded as unsocial. Up country at Dassa Zoumé I tried to have just one steward-cook, but a gardener-watchman was also needed, one of his principal tasks being to wait in turn at the sole village well at night to fill a barrel of water for the day's use.

Household servants were usually men, though they might all be called 'boys'. They were not normally girls or women, and one friend who went to the West Indies where women were employed as house servants, found temptation in the 'boy' who was a girl. But in Africa even male 'boys' could become intimate and present problems.

We were gathering together for an annual conference and a colleague arrived from a country station. Rather bluffly I inquired, 'How's your soul?'

He poured out his troubles without further invitation. It was his 'boy', a man in his twenties, slim and with fair brown skin. He waited on his master devotedly, brought him tea in bed, returned with hot water for shaving, put up the mosquito net, made the bed, and stayed around while master was dressing.

'He looked in the mirror while I was sitting at the dressing table, standing behind me. His brown skin was fresh, newly washed and lightly powdered. He was beautiful. I leaned back and he pressed on me. Then he began to caress me, and I liked it. He was kind and comforting, and I had been so lonely.'

'You didn't go any further?'

'No, but I felt like it, and I know he would have agreed. What shall I do? What can I do?'

'You must get away, change your station. You are due for furlough, and six months in England does us much good. Perhaps you will meet a nice girl. We all need a companion.'

He went on leave and later got married, but whether that was for the best might be debatable.

* * * * *

For those of us who were happily married there was companionship and sexual fulfilment. We enjoyed books recommended by Weatherhead and others, like Marie Stopes on *Married Love* and Helena Wright on *The Sex Factor in Marriage*, which showed that there was more than one so-called 'missionary position'.

There were also the trials of long separations because of the children. I was away in Africa for two-and-a-half years on my own during the war. I wrote home every day but replies took three months. Letters came out by boat to Dahomey but then were returned, also by boat, to Dakar where there was the censorship office for all of French West Africa, then back to Dahomey.

Children later complained that their fathers were away from home, but so were millions in the armed forces, and some never returned. A French teacher in Dahomey, Louis Guichard, was absent from France for years. His wife had gone home pregnant at the beginning of the war, but because of the German occupation of France he was unable to see his son till the boy was six years old.

Having children was always a problem, even in peacetime, because of the dangerous climate of West Africa. A couple living in the Ataké house had been married longer than us, and seemed to have no thought of children. But when Mary announced her pregnancy, late in 1937, due for completion on furlough the following year, our neighbour's wife was surprised, delighted, and began to think of changing plans. When she and her husband went on leave they took a French ship from Cotonou and travelled through France to England, spending a few days holiday in Paris. Three months later came news that she was expecting a baby, and the wise Demoiselles at the girls' school said with one voice, 'It will be a Parisian.'

12. BLACK MAN'S GRAVE

A colleague in Porto Novo had been notorious for conflicts both with traditional Voodoo and with African catechists and ministers, and his exploits were discussed for several years before I arrived. He will be called Jerome Legrand, a Belgian, of Calvinistic background, who was uneasy with the tolerance of the English mission, as he saw it.

Due to shortages of French-speaking European workers, Jerome was given oversight both of the town church and of smaller chapels in neighbouring villages. Early one January he cycled on a Sunday morning ten kilometres to the village of Méridjonou, to be with simple country people, as he thought them to be. Cycling was good exercise, appealing to his Protestant work ethic, and it seemed nearer to the people than riding by car. But the road was dusty and bumpy, and in the twenties and thirties there were no tarred or cobbled roads outside Porto Novo town. Motor lorries raised clouds of dust as they passed through villages and the countryside.

Jerome usually wore shorts and open-necked shirt, but on this morning, to conform with Sunday custom, he had put on a white suit and black tie. He arrived sweating and soiled, and leant his bicycle against the chapel wall in the village. It was little more than a mud shelter, not much bigger than a house, with open windows and thatched roof without a ceiling. Jerome noticed a tiny hut next door, but for the moment paid no attention to it.

The village catechist, Daniel, was in charge of religious services and also acted as monitor, teaching children reading and writing in French. The government did not control or recognize such independent village schools, since official policy was to concentrate on a few high grade schools in the towns. Strictly, private village schools, Protestant and Catholic, were illegal. But they had been long established and were demanded by the village people; administrators ignored their existence and the absence of qualified teachers.

Daniel met Jerome and bowed, but his superior did not offer to shake hands. The two men talked for some minutes and then a boy struck a rusty iron rim of an old car wheel which was hanging outside, to call people to church. Inside there were no pews, but boxes to sit on, and a small table at the far end was covered with a cloth and had on it a jar of flowers, a pot of violet ink and a pen. The congregation was composed mostly of children, with a few men and women.

Jerome conducted a formal service, speaking in French to Daniel's interpretations. There were hymns and readings from Goungbé hymn books and Bible. But Jerome struggled with prayers and a short sermon, which was an exposition of a parable. Daniel translated, and people seemed interested when he made a long explanation of what the white man had said, or intended.

After the service Jerome examined the children and listened to high-pitched and mangled French recitations of fables from La Fontaine. He was trying to learn patience, and gave brief thanks to each child. The girls, dressed in short khaki frocks, were not so advanced as the boys, he thought, yet some seemed bright and attentive to his every move. He had a feeling that they were weighing him up, with a view to help for future entrance to the Porto Novo girls' school. Parents then demanded to know when they could have a proper school at Méridjonou, with desks and books, and Jerome spoke of the difficulty of getting qualified teachers for village schools, He spoke of the shortage of funds, which would have to come from local fees, and then he cut off discussion.

Leaving the chapel, Jerome turned to look at the little hut next door that he had noticed on arrival. It was set back a little from the road, and in front was a small clay mound of a Legba with a wooden phallus. Behind it the thatched shrine had painted walls, and inside by stooping down he could see a low earthen platform on which rested a clay bowl containing oval stones.

'What is this?' he demanded sternly.

'It is a village vodoun,' replied Daniel.

'Vodoun? That's a nasty thing. How long has it been here?'

'Since last month.'

'It is an insult to us,' declared Jerome, 'putting a Vodoun, and that object, next to our church. Why have you not prevented it?'

'I have tried, sir,' Daniel replied, 'but it is their land. Ours was only loaned, as a concession from the village chief to parents who wanted a school.'

'But our chapel was there first, was it not? They will annoy us and interrupt our work. The Zangbeto will come out with their ridiculous masks and horns. And those Legba objects are indecent. But we shall show them that they cannot attack the religion of the white man. I shall report it to the Chef de Canton. Better still, I'll help him in his work.'

Jerome went forward and kicked the metal stand in front of the Legba mound, which fell down with a clatter. Then he tore the phallic wood from its base, kicked it when it resisted his tug, and flung it far into the bush. Daniel watched anxiously, but when Jerome bent down to go inside the little hut he pulled at his sleeve.

'Do not enter there, Monsieur. It is dangerous, taboo. Only the priests can go in.'

'That is their nonsense, superstition. You ought to know that.'

'I do know it, sir. But there are thunder-stones inside, fallen from heaven, from So, as the people believe. They will not like you touching them. It is black man's religion.'

'Then they must learn the superior faith of the whites,' retorted Jerome fiercely. He crouched down and crept under the low roof of the shrine. He picked up some oval stones and weighed them in his hand. Then he backed out and shouted to the village people.

The group of parents had scattered and only a few women were pounding meal beside their huts nearby. They heard the white man's cry in French but did not understand it.

'Vodoun is superstition. These stones are nothing. Do you hear?' called Jerome.

Nobody had moved when he threw the Legba stick away, and they did not follow his words. But when Jerome held up the thunder-stones to show them, and put them in his pocket, the women stopped pounding, and there was a gasp of astonishment, followed by an ominous quiet.

94

Jerome was pleased with himself for having demonstrated so clearly the superior power of Europe. He already planned to send the thunder-stones to the national museum in Brussels and had begun to formulate a label, 'Objects of Voodoo from heathen Africa, supposed thunder-stones, probably prehistoric axes,' with his name as donor.

He cycled off without a glance at the ashen pallor of Daniel, or the children running home after their parents. But the excitement and the long hot ride at midday gave Jerome a headache and returning fever, and he went early to bed.

* * * * *

At dawn next day there was a quiet but urgent tapping at John Watson's door at the seminary. When it was opened, Paul Hountodji, minister in training, came inside, followed by a thin, shaking man.

'He is from Méridjonou,' Paul told John. 'There is much trouble. Pasteur Legrand was there yesterday, did you know?'

'No, he's at the Ataké house. What's he been up to?'

Paul interpreted the man's account of Jerome's actions and went on, to John's surprise and concern, 'The white man left peaceably but as night fell the Vodoun priests of So in full costume and the Zangbeto society came out and made a great noise. They rounded up the church members, parents and children, when they could find them, and the catechist Daniel. They herded them all into the church building and shut the door, nailing it up, and fixing thick palm branches across the side windows so that nobody could get out. That would be impossible anyway, for the men surrounded the chapel, blowing horns, shaking rattles, uttering curses and threats. Then they started digging graves and shouting that Daniel would only come out to be buried, with the church members.'

'Good heavens! How long did that go on?'

'All night, and it is still continuing. This man is a friend of Daniel's. He saw what happened through the trees, slipped off and walked all the way here in the dark.'

John got dressed and then, with Paul and the man, went to the Ataké house to find Jerome. He had been for an early morning walk to clear his head. When he saw the delegation, he asked what was the matter; he grew pale, but his face stiffened with resolve.

'I shall go to Méridjonou,' he declared.

'No, sir,' pleaded Paul. 'That would make it worse. The Vodoun priests and Zangbeto are there, and they will not let you get near the church or talk to the people inside. If they attack a white man, there will be terrible palaver with the government, and all our work will be in danger.'

'Did you actually take the stones away?' asked John.

'They are in my room. My trophies,' replied Jerome defiantly.

'Please, sir, they must go back,' pleaded Paul, 'or our people will die.'

'Your pride, or their life,' said John to Jerome. He turned to Paul and asked, 'What do you suggest can be done?'

'I think we must first try the King of the Night. He is in charge of all the Vodouns and societies in the district.'

'Ah, yes. Shall I come?'

'No, I think I must go. I have a friend in the palace, and I must take the stones, and a present.'

Jerome listened, disagreeing with the idea of a present but unable to suggest another course. He handed over the thunder-stones reluctantly, while John told his cook to prepare a meal for the man from Méridjonou. Then they sat down to await Paul's return.

Paul came back after a couple of hours, with downcast face.

'I could not see the king,' he reported. 'He is busy, or sick, or away. I got his officer to accept the stones, after much argument. But Monsieur Legrand has troubled the Zangbeto here at Ataké, throwing water over them, and he has spoken ill of the Vodoun priests at different times, and the king is aware of this. His sergeant did not tell me directly, but I gathered that the king would let the priests frighten the people, short of killing them, which he would not allow, to show that native customs must not be interfered with. It touches his own authority. Through evasive answers I deduced that nothing would be done for a week, perhaps two. Our people may not die of fright, but nobody will be able to take them food or drink, and they may well faint or starve to death.'

'Perhaps then we must try to use some influence with the government,' said John. 'It likes to think it is in control, despite the traditional power of the King of the Night. I can ask a friend at the treasury, and he may know the district officer in charge of Méridjonou. It is worth attempting. I'll go and see.'

This was done, and work started through official and unofficial channels. But it took two days, while the Vodoun priests and Zangbeto at Méridjonou kept watch, dancing day and night round the chapel and letting no one enter or leave. The King of the Night would not tell them to stop, but after a time he agreed to permit a diversion. One of his officials called the priests to a grand evening sacrifice, and another slipped into the little shrine and replaced the thunder-stones on the altar. The watch was broken, and the children and parents climbed out of the chapel windows and rushed away in the dark, to be revived and fed by friends.

'Your Belgian colleague is a menace,' said Watson's friend at the treasury. 'He ought to be up country, where the people are quieter. The soldiers say that the regions beyond old Dahomey were "pacified" more easily than the coastal warriors. You have work up north, I believe. They might accept a dictator there, and he could learn patience. You must do something to get him transferred.'

'We have our Synod coming on,' replied John. 'That could move him, if it was done discreetly.'

* * * * *

A further conflict for Jerome Legrand, and more troublesome to him personally, arose with the church at Ouézoumé and its African minister. James Johnson (I think was his name) came from that part of old German Togo which had been incorporated into British-ruled Gold Coast during the First World War. But he had relatives on the French side and came to work in Togo-Dahomey, which was part of the church's French West Africa district. He was appointed minister at Porto Novo church, but under the direction of Jerome Legrand as superintendent of the town and country circuit, although Jerome was a younger man and was not a Methodist.

Jerome could not resist interfering, or asserting his formal seniority. At the harvest festival Monday sale he arrived early and forbade any attempts at dancing, which he regarded as immoral. He strode back to Ataké before James Johnson arrived, and members complained to their own pastor about this meddling by the white man. Some young people then went and danced outside the Ataké house late at night, and Jerome threw water over them from the upstairs bathroom, as he had done over the Zangbeto.

Next morning James Johnson went to Ataké to protest, complaining that his own authority had been undermined. He reminded Jerome that the first division of the church under Arnett had resulted in the founding of the Eleja church, and the Elejas were still active and seeking to attract our members. Jerome was surprised but insistent on his own higher authority. He kept Johnson standing and addressed him as 'tu'. There were high words between the two men, which were heard by the Ataké servants. They could not understand much French, but they reported on a violent quarrel. Johnson marched away in temper, and the news spread abroad.

Next day James Johnson was taken seriously ill. Native medicines had no effect, and he was rushed to the small military hospital. His fever rose without stop and he died at the end of the week. The sickness was not diagnosed – perhaps it was polio, which was hardly recognized at that time – but church and town were shocked. They were used to sudden deaths, which took away black and white people equally quickly, but in the houses and streets ugly rumours started and spread. Nothing was secret and the quarrel of the two ministers became public and grew in the telling.

It was widely believed that nobody died by accident. There were many known poisons, and every traditional Dahomean believed in sorcery and witchcraft. 'An enemy had done this thing', and thoughts turned to Jerome

Legrand. True, he was a pastor and a white man, and he ought to have been above such things and outside the range of African life. But he was known for his zeal and quick temper. Also he was neither French nor English, and rumour held that he came from some black forest in the mountains.

Gossip ran through Porto Novo, with talk of the mysterious powers of the whites. If they knew how to practise it, 'white man's magic' could be even more subtle and dangerous than black man's. Where did Europeans get their powerful weapons and machines from, if not from magic? Did they not speak of devils and Satan in their sacred book? Some people knew of other books which dealt with witchcraft and devouring the souls of children, which explained high infant mortality. European pamphlets on magic and secret potions and Cabbalistic mysteries were even now advertised at high prices in Lagos newspapers.

Accusations grew rapidly and church members became worried. Not just the unpopular Jerome but the whole church and its schools which tried to raise society above pagan superstitions were affected. A delegation came to see Paul Hountodji at the seminary; he told John Watson, and he went with their tale to Jerome.

'I know it's nonsense,' said John, 'but they are very concerned for you, for all of us, and for the churches and schools.'

Jerome was depressed, feeling unwell and uneasy at the vague clouds of rumour. 'What can I do?' he asked, with rare humility.

'The members suggest that the only way to scotch the rumours is for you to join the mourners at Johnson's funeral, and attend the whole ceremony with his family.'

'When is it to be? The burial must be soon in this climate. I am surprised it has not been arranged already. I have been waiting to hear about it.'

'The body has been preserved at the hospital mortuary. Now the relatives are insisting that it must be taken home to the family graves in the Gold Coast.'

'But that's two hundred miles away, beyond Dahomey and Togo.'

'About a hundred,' replied John, 'the other side of the French Togo frontier. I've told you the opinion of the relatives and Paul, but now I must insist that I do not agree at all. I have also seen the Demoiselles at the girls' school, and they share my view that it would be better to live things down here. You had nothing to do with this illness and death, even if you had disagreed with Johnson. Everybody in the church and the educated community knows that really. To go to a distant funeral might rebound on you and suggest gloating over the catastrophe.'

'I shall go,' declared Jerome. 'Perhaps I have found out something about native mentality, despite what people think. They give great attention to funerals. It would be far worse for me to be absent, and suggest callousness or malevolence. I shall go, as colleague and superintendent minister. That is proper to my position, and it will show concern and participation in the ceremonies, however distant they may be.'

* * * * *

A long black car, with several others following, drew up at the Ataké house two days later, in the morning. Jerome was ready, and Watson had come to see him off. The chauffeur of the main car opened the door for Jerome, who stared into the back and hesitated, but with a shrug of resolution he got in, squeezing himself closely against the door.

Watson saw a slight movement of salutation from another passenger on the far side of the car, but now to his horror he discerned, in the middle of the back seat the stiff form and greyish-black face of the dead James Johnson. The body was upright, in a sitting position, fully dressed in a white suit, with a high white clerical collar under the face and a large sun helmet pulled low down. John half moved to draw his colleague back, but he was too late. The chauffeur had shut the door, slipped into the front seat, and engaged first gear; and the car rolled away along the cobbled road.

When Jerome had agreed to go to the funeral in the Gold Coast, he expected to see a hearse with a coffin and other cars behind. Now he found himself riding beside a corpse, and half thought of refusing to go. But a strong sense of discipline, for himself as well as others, and a wish to right any wrongs and dispel rumours, nerved him for the journey. The body of the

100

dead minister sat beside him. The face was shrunken and flabby, but it could hardly be seen between the helmet and collar. There was a strong smell of preservative, and Jerome forced himself as near as possible to the car door. But he could not avoid brushing occasionally against the body, as the car dodged goats and dogs and turned corners on its way through the town.

First there were the cobblestones, and then a stretch of cemented road by the lagoon, which separated the capital of the colony from the coastline. There was no bridge over the lagoon at that time, and a piece of rusty railway line, hanging on a post, was struck several times to summon a ferry from the far side of the water. There was a long wait while a large flat-bottomed boat was poled across the shallow muddy lagoon to take two cars. At the other side there was a further wait for the rest of the cars to join the cortege.

The cars drove westwards along the coastal road in the growing heat. There were avenues of coconut palms and casuarina trees, and in the distance Atlantic rollers could sometimes be heard breaking on the shore. The way was stony and dusty, made of laterite and gravel, but it ran fairly straight through the port of Cotonou and on to the frontiers. At another time Jerome would have enjoyed the ride, but the air felt like heat from an oven and the company depressed him. The relative sat on the other side of the corpse, but he knew little French and hardly spoke after a brief greeting.

There was a stop at midday to buy food from a wayside stall. Jerome got out to stretch his legs and his companions brought him slices of plaintain fried in greasy palm oil, which he disliked but ate because he was hungry, and he was also given a drink of coconut milk. In early afternoon he dozed, until the cars stopped and someone pulled at his shoulder.

They had passed the frontier of Dahomey into Togo, since both were French colonies without customs posts, and formal nods from soldiers had enabled them to continue. Now they reached the borders of French Togo and British Gold Coast. The mourning family came from these regions and had friends at both French and British offices, to whom they passed over gifts of French tobacco and scent. They excused James Johnson from getting out of the car. He was a man of God, they said, tired and asleep, and it would be kindness not to wake him. They did not say he was dead. His pass was presented and stamped.

There was some trouble over Jerome Legrand. He was a Belgian and a puzzle to officials who scanned the unusual passport. On the Togo side he was made to fill in forms in triplicate. At the Gold Coast there was a further question of paying a deposit for Jerome's admission to the country and repatriation fare back home if it were needed. Jerome had not thought of this and had only a few notes in his wallet. It took more brotherly backslappings, and perhaps bribes, from his companions to get him passed.

'Make you drive on left,' called the guard as they changed sides of the road for driving in British territory.

The family town was not far from the frontier, and the funeral procession arrived in the late afternoon, to find a large crowd assembled. Both the telegraph and talking drums had spread news of this important death, and other drums were beating all round as the cortege drew up at the ancestral compound.

There were greetings and lamentations from all the family, dressed in their best clothes. But time was pressing, the day was declining, and salutations were cut short to allow for the obligatory photograph before dark. Benches had been brought from the church and armchairs for the most important or elderly persons as they were arranged in rank.

Surrounded by relatives and friends in black suits, gorgeous coloured cloths and best mourning dresses, the body of James Johnson was lifted out of the car. It had stiffened into the sitting position, but it was set down in the central chair, in white suit and clerical collar, but with topee removed, for a last family picture.

Jerome had been almost ignored in the family scramble for the best positions, but he suddenly realized the importance of the photograph. This was what he had come for, and he had earned his place by enduring the long and unpleasant journey. He edged near to the centre of the family group and people gave way, recognizing his right to be there and glad to have a white minister in the midst of the picture. He stood behind his old colleague and adversary, and tried to keep a straight face in the glare of the setting sun. For once Jerome wished he had a clerical collar, which he had always resisted wearing, or even a black gown. But his creased white suit was acceptable, and he felt he had made atonement.

There followed a very long service in church and burial in a cemetery by lamplight. At the grave Jerome was shocked to hear the family elders and another minister reading prayers and then addressing the corpse, telling it not to come back but to rest in peace. As they left the burial ground, everybody went away quickly, leaving Jerome to come out last, and the mourners pulled a branch from a tree over the path to prevent the spirit following them.

Back in the town Jerome was hungry and bought some bananas, while an old woman beckoned him into a house and gave him a mat to sleep on the floor. But he was pestered by mosquitoes, and when at last he had got to sleep, being worn out by the long day, he was wakened by a boy with bowls of rice and chicken in palm oil. They had not forgotten him, but it had taken time to get food organized.

Jerome returned to Porto Novo with one of the cars next day, and went to bed with fever and a high temperature. He consoled himself with the thought that he had done his duty, but he also began to hope that the Synod might station him away from the town, to up country regions where people were supposed to be simpler.

13. TO EAST AND WEST

The Synod, the major business meeting of the Wesleyan Methodist Church, was held annually at the end of December or early in January. In pre-colonial times Methodist work in Porto Novo, together with its small Dahomean and Togolese offshoots, came under the Yoruba (later Western Nigerian) mission, and the joint synod was usually held in Lagos. Then in the 1890s British and French government officials drew lines on almost blank maps, defining the boundaries of their respective spheres and separating Dahomey from Nigeria. The frontiers often followed rivers and cut across racial and linguistic groups, the official languages, English and French, being imposed on their administrative areas.

Despite governmental barriers, the Methodist synod in western Nigeria continued for some thirty years to include Dahomey and Togo. But there were special problems for Methodist work on the French side. More French-speaking missionaries were needed, and it was felt that Dahomean affairs were not fully understood or catered for in Lagos, but changes were being planned. A young and energetic missionary, W. J. Platt, dominated Methodist work in French-speaking West Africa from 1916 to 1930 (he died in 1993 aged 100). In 1921 he recruited a French Methodist minister, Paul Wood, at the Conference of the French Methodist Church, and in 1923 the Paris Evangelical Mission lent two more Frenchmen to Dahomey, Antoine Léthel and Alexandre Westphal. With this help Platt planned to form an independent French West Africa district, and perhaps begin the boys' school in Porto Novo, but developments in the French Ivory Coast to the west changed this plan.

When I arrived in 1933 Westphal and Wood had returned to France, though the latter was to come back to Dahomey during the Second World War. Léthel had returned to Porto Novo from the Ivory Coast for a time but also went back to France. Since he had a large family and France encouraged such prolific parents, he was exempted from military service. He was a charming man, whose knowledge of English seemed to have been gathered chiefly from the Authorized Version of the Bible and the novels of P. G. Wodehouse. His conversation was sprinkled with words like 'scaly' or 'spiky', or phrases such as 'fate creeps up behind you with a length of lead piping.'

While Dahomey was attached to Nigeria, Platt attended the Synod with one of his new recruits. It was still related ten years later, how they went in 1923 by launch to Lagos, Platt taking Westphal with him. They arrived in the evening after dark, were met at the wharf, hurried to a synod meeting already in progress and put in vacant front seats. It was in a hall at the boys' school where several ministers, white and black, were sitting on a platform facing a large and colourful African audience. A speaker was holding forth on the virtues of abstinence and the dangers of drinking imported or locally brewed beer.

Westphal did not understand much English, and he said to his companion in a loud whisper, 'Vot'e say, Platt?'

'He is talking about temperance,' Platt answered.

'Vot is dat? 'E speak about beer?'

'He says you should not drink it.'

'Beer?' exclaimed Westphal in a loud voice. 'Beer? I like eet. I drink eet.'

There was shock on the platform, and giggles from the African congregation, and Platt quickly got his companion out of the room.

The policy of the Nigerian Methodist mission was strictly teetotal, as was that of Methodist churches in Britain at that time. But in the French-speaking mission there were more relaxed attitudes and practices, which continued during the following decades.

There were also different customs of dress, with much more formality on the British side than on the French. One Chairman, director of the mission in Nigeria in the 1920s, had served in India, and he and his wife tried to continue or impose Indian imperial practices in Africa. When they went up country, into 'the bush', they would stay at government rest houses and always change into evening dress for dinner, even on their own and in the most remote places. They thought they were on a civilizing mission which required formal dress, keeping up appearances, not letting the side down. On the French side, I only knew of one English missionary couple who, on their own in the bush, changed into evening dress for dinner into the 1930s and '40s.

Most missionary delegates to the Synod were lodged in mission houses, or given camp beds in classrooms of the boys' and girls' schools, which were empty during the Christmas holidays. The Chairman invited his colleagues, European but not African, to formal dinners at his house on the Marina. African delegates, ministerial and lay, were given hospitality with their compatriots and friends elsewhere in Lagos.

Platt and Westphal were invited to the dinners, at which ordained ministers were supposed to wear black suits and clerical collars and ladies long dresses with sleeves, despite the heat. Platt had been in Lagos before, since 1916, and had a black suit, but he had forgotten to warn Westphal. The chairman's wife stood at the door of the dining-room, stiffly corseted and wearing a long black sleeved dress, and she looked affronted at Westphal in his crumpled white suit. Platt explained that he was a benighted foreigner, and the excuse passed. It was suspected that peculiar customs existed among the French. But a rebellious young English missionary also came in white, and explained that his black suit had got mouldy in his bush station. He was reprimanded by the chairman's wife for not wearing black regularly in the evenings and for not training his boy to brush the suit daily. He was forbidden to enter the room for dinner and sent back to his lodgings, without a meal.

Greetings were formal and it was rare even to shake hands, especially with ladies. Westphal caused surprise because the French, of course, shook hands on every possible occasion. Women rarely kissed one another in public, and the modern habit of men and women kissing all and sundry would have been regarded as promiscuous. In the universities later kissing became more general, of Africans by Europeans as well, which to an earlier generation, in church or state, would have been inconceivable.

There might be concessions to national customs. At Synod, in French West Africa in 1935, a French lady invited some of us to tea. Anxious to do the right thing, she asked how many teaspoonfuls of tea to put in the pot. 'One, or one-and-a-half, Messieurs?'

With one voice we English replied, 'Madame, one for each person and one for the pot.'

She was suitably shocked but no doubt thought it was one of those strange English jokes. The tea she gave us was poor stuff.

* * * * *

Separation of the Dahomean churches from Nigeria and formation of an independent French West Africa district of the Methodist Church was hastened by a completely new and unexpected development in the far west. In 1913 a self-styled Prophet, William Wadé Harris, came from Liberia into French-ruled Ivory Coast, preaching repentance and conversion, destruction of 'fetishes' and worship of the one true God. He preached in English, or his own Grebo language, and used interpreters. One of them, Victor Tano, was my own interpreter for a time twenty years later.

Harris had great success: it is probable that over a hundred thousand people accepted his teachings, and others were influenced. He travelled along the lagoon areas of the southern Ivory Coast and into the Gold Coast (Ghana). But French government officials were alarmed at these mass movements. The First World War was raging in Europe, there had been battles with Germans in Africa, and there were fears of independent or separatist movements among the indigenous populations. At the end of 1914 Harris was expelled from French territory and returned to Liberia, where he lived till his death in 1929.

Harris told his converts to build churches, buy Bibles, and wait for the coming of other Christian preachers and missionaries who would continue his work. For ten years they waited, with only occasional encouragement from visiting lay preachers from the Gold Coast, who spoke in English or a Gold Coast language. The Bibles Harris's converts bought were often in English also, and there was great dismay when the government imposed the French language on all religious work. By the Protocol of St Germain, in 1919 freedom of conscience for all forms of religion was guaranteed in the French, British and other empires, but in 1922 a decree from Paris ruled that in French territory no churches might be established or collections taken without governmental permission. More pointedly, only French, Latin, or an African vernacular language might be used at religious services.

This ruling brought despair to the Wesleyan Methodists in the Gold Coast, who had been trying to help the Ivory Coast Harrist converts with English-speaking preachers. They saw their influence being taken away, either by Roman Catholics or by independent Harrist churches. A missionary at Cape Coast appealed for guidance to W. J. Platt, who was on leave in England, and in September 1923 Platt called at the Ivory Coast on his way back to Dahomey. Always careful of authority, Platt wrote to the Lieutenant-Governor of the Ivory Coast, whom he knew personally, promising that French or African languages would be used in all churches, but asking for a period of grace for the changeover. He encouraged church workers to learn and use French, and told them that French-speaking ministers and catechists would be sent to the Ivory Coast from Dahomey.

Platt sent a report to the Mission House in London, suggesting that the Ivory Coast be included in his proposed French West Africa district. This was viewed with some hesitation in England, since the missionary income for that year was £86,000 down on its target and new schemes were not welcome. Nevertheless the Lagos synod approved the plan for a new district, which was agreed by the British Methodist Conference in July 1924.

Platt then went back to the Ivory Coast, to study the situation more thoroughly, and he was amazed at the vast crowds that welcomed him in the towns and many villages. He travelled by canoe, car and train, and was received everywhere with bands, flags and great crowds, and he saw mud and stone churches that had been erected.

Back in Dahomey Platt sent his new French colleague, Antoine Léthel, to the Ivory Coast, along with ten French-speaking Dahomean catechists. They were soon followed by Wood, Westphal, and further catechists. Wood and Léthel composed an appeal to Protestant pastors and teachers in France, but replies were limited among the minority Huguenots of France, and over the years French-speakers came to the Ivory Coast and Dahomey from Switzerland, Holland and Britain.

Platt moved his headquarters to Abidjan, capital of the Ivory Coast, in 1925, and he stayed there till 1930, when he suddenly retired to England, discouraged by the lack of support which he thought should have come from the home church. His departure was a great shock to his colleagues, European and African, but the Togolese minister, Edwin Gaba, wrote that, if the French no longer suspected the Wesleyan mission of being an English agency 'to entice the Natives away to British rule', it was due to Platt's prudence.

Platt was followed by other 'Chairmen' of the district, French and British in turn. The new district had a long title in French, being known as La Mission Protestante d'Afrique Occidentale Française (Société des Missions Wesleyennes de Londres). In English lists addresses were given as Mission Protestante (or Méthodiste) in Dahomey, Togo, or Ivory Coast, via France, postage 2½d.

* * * * *

From being at the edge of the much larger Yoruba mission to the east, the Dahomean churches were now overshadowed by great developments in the west, and the new French West Africa Methodist district tended to be dominated by Ivory Coast affairs. Protestant Dahomey, however, was not a poor relative; it had become a missionary church. From a history of struggle to maintain its witness amid the surrounding animism and polytheism, the Dahomean and Togolese churches were now sending their own pastors and catechists to work in the harvests of the Ivory Coast. Although they did not speak Ivory Coast languages at first, and their chief advantage was knowledge of French, Dahomeans helped in putting these new languages into writing and beginning translations of the Bible, a task which is still continuing.

My own first experience of a Synod of the French West Africa district was at the end of December 1933. It was held in the seminary at Porto Novo. Delegates, mostly missionaries and African ministers, came by road from Togo and by sea from the Ivory Coast. There were ordinations in Ouézoumé church of three African probationer ministers. No African ministers had yet come from the Ivory Coast, since the Methodist church there was barely ten years old.

Sessions of Synod met in the seminary classrooms, and private committees in mission houses. The chairman was Robert Howett, an Englishman stationed at Abidjan in the Ivory Coast, and there were other British and French missionaries, two Swiss and one Dutch. Older African ministers were Edwin Gaba, D. Hodonou Loko and J. B. Lawson, all of whom had served in the Ivory Coast but now were back in churches in Dahomey and Togo.

One veteran minister was Papa Henry, the first Dahomean to be ordained into the Wesleyan Methodist ministry. In the early years of the twentieth century, the Rev Gabriel Okou Henry had been one of the translators of the Allada (Goungbé) whole Bible, which was used in southern Dahomey. But now he was an old man who lounged at the back of the synod classroom, took off his shoes and slept through much of the proceedings. His grandson, Harry Henry, was then a student of mine at the seminary, and much later he became Chairman of the Dahomey (Bénin) Methodist district (he died in 1999). The Henrys had links with Nigeria, and spoke English as well as French, while Edwin Gaba, who came from what had been German Togo, knew German, French and some English.

The cosmopolitan connections of various African church leaders gave them a wider outlook than the purely French concerns to which some government officials would have liked to restrict their subjects. Dahomean church leaders often had links with kinsmen in Nigeria, and Ivory Coast people with relatives in the Gold Coast or Liberia. During the Second World War these connections meant that Africans in French-ruled territory were often more in touch and in sympathy with Britain and her allies than those French administrators who followed the directives of the Vichy government. For much of the twentieth century there were tensions of various kinds, due to language and political links, by which the Methodist churches in French West Africa were affected, as will be seen later.

I had been teaching biblical and church subjects, and also some French language, history and geography, in the seminary at Porto Novo. The Synod, in a private committee which I, as a probationer, was not entitled to attend, decided to transfer me to the junior seminary at Dabou in the Ivory Coast. The principal of the Porto Novo seminary, Herbert Bishop, had returned from leave and he, with John Watson and Paul Hountodji, formed its teaching staff. At Dabou there was a Swiss minister-teacher, but he preferred to go into evangelistic church work, and I took over as principal, with Donald Ching as my colleague.

Since this book is about Dahomey, my two years in the Ivory Coast, one at Dabou and another in a vast area of forest and lagoons in the Grand Lahou 'circuit', will not be described. It is enough to say that, having left Porto Novo at the beginning of 1934, I returned there, after furlough and marriage, in 1936.

14. A TEAR FOR FRIENDSHIP

Porto Novo was the capital of the colony of Dahomey and a centre of the Protestant church and teaching work, but there were many other town and village churches, some of them only thinly supported in the thirties and forties. There were small chapels of fishing communities along the Atlantic seaboard, and a new medium-sized church in the seaport of Cotonou, where there are several churches today. Then, there were little groups along the coast into the colony of Togo, where the French Evangelical Mission of Paris was also at work.

Towards the interior of the country there was the great block of the real Dahomey, the ancient kingdom of the 'snake's belly', with its capital at Abomey. Here Catholics and Protestants had few followers, since the old royal and traditional religion, called by outsiders 'fetishism' or 'juju' or 'paganism', held sway. Ancient thatched palaces and tombs were preserved, and there were some survivors of the famous female warriors, 'Amazons', who had fought fiercely against the French at the end of the nineteenth century. With an administrator friend I once had a meal with the descendant of the ancient kings, now Chef de Canton, and met some Amazons, thin but respected old ladies.

A single track railway ran from Cotonou through central Dahomey and as far as Parakou, over halfway up the colony. Christian African railway workers, in the twenties and thirties, had founded small chapels beyond Abomey, and there were moderately strong church centres at Dassa Zoumé, Savé and Kilibo. Dassa became the church organizational post for the central region of the country, and I visited it with Mary in 1937 and was stationed there, with responsibility for the supervision of the whole district, in 1943-4. First impressions of Dassa may be mentioned here.

The railway service was slow and uncomfortable, most engines being fuelled with wood and carriages having wooden seats. But there had recently been introduced a fast service of small passenger coaches, with an engine run on diesel oil, for which the system was cleared of slow passenger and goods trains. Called the Micheline, the rail car service went twice a week, and in 1937 we travelled by car to Cotonou, to join the Micheline for the two hour journey to Dassa Zoumé.

As the train went from Cotonou northwards into the interior the vegetation changed. The innumerable oil palms of the coastal regions gave way to forest with towering trees, and then to open plains and savanna. Here in scrubby undergrowth were scattered small trees, some of shea butter, while huge granite rocks and occasional domed hills rose above them.

'Look, there's baboon climbing up a rock,' I said.

'It's the first wild animal I've seen in a year in Africa,' replied Mary, gazing at it.

When the train drew near Dassa, it entered a wide plain and swung round in a semi-circle, skirting a range of granite hills. Dassa clustered under the highest hill, which was crowned with a great split granite boulder, hanging over the village where houses and shops were lively with people. At the railway station there were crowds shouting and pushing to meet friends or collect luggage, and we were met by the catechist. It was only a five-minute walk to the mission house and we took a sandy path passing the village well to the bungalow ahead. This building was low and wide, and made of concrete blocks on a granite foundation. There was a central lounge, with large bedrooms on either side, a study-office beyond them and a kitchen at the back. Beneath a roof of asbestos sheets all was clean and cool.

To the side of the mission house there was a small mud chapel, though by 1944 a shell of granite blocks outlined a new church, which was enlarged and completed later. Beyond the chapel was the catechist's mud house, and an open palm-covered shelter which served as a school. In the surrounding villages there were larger churches, most at that time with mud walls and thatched roofs but later to be rebuilt or replaced with larger constructions.

We had a happy time, cycling out to the villages and doing our own cleaning and cooking in the staff house, for the climate was cooler than at the coast and we had more energy. The village people saluted Mary as 'Mother', which seemed premature, though afterwards we recognized their perception.

* * * * *

112

In 1944, I returned to Dassa Zoumé for a longer period while waiting to take over from Paul Wood at the Porto Novo seminary, which will be noted later. After the January synod I was accompanied to Dassa by English colleagues Harold Stacey and Ernest Partner (District Chairman and Secretary), who had come over from the Ivory Coast to synod in Dahomey. The three of us went by road in the Dassa van and, since at that time the roads beyond Cotonou were all made of red earth, we were soon covered in dust.

We arrived at Dassa in the evening, looking like Red Indians, and the first concern was to get baths and change all our clothes. There were only low round zinc baths, and all water had to be brought by the gardener in a long empty oil drum from the village well.

Amos Djossou, a newly ordained minister from Porto Novo, had control of the district of Dassa. He also acted as companion and interpreter, since he knew the dialect of the Yoruba language which was dominant in much of central Dahomey.

Amos was a splendid worker, and in due course he and I travelled together by car and foot all round Dassa and Kilibo, and into the northern parts of the country beyond the railhead at Parakou towards Djougou and Natitingou. Others had pioneered work in the far north of the colony which we were unable to develop, and eventually American missions took over much of it.

'When you have bathed and rested', Amos told us, 'we should pay some courtesy calls, perhaps in the evening, tomorrow and the next day.'

'Is there much high society?' we asked.

'First of all there is the town chief, and we must ask to see his horse.'

'I thought horses could not survive here,' I objected, 'because of the sleeping sickness.'

'You will see. Then perhaps next day you should call on the Catholics.'

'Are we on good terms, then?'

'At certain hours of the day.'

Next evening after tea the three white men, with Amos as leader and interpreter, set out to visit the chief of Dassa town. The climate was more temperate than in the sticky coastal regions, and an avenue of acacia trees gave shade down to the village well. More trees, with brilliant red flowers and long black pods hanging from the branches, lined dusty roads through the town, and we enjoyed the cool walk across a grassy plain.

'What about this horse?' I asked Amos. 'Don't horses get ill here, as they do at the coast?'

'They do.'

'Then how does the chief's horse survive?'

'Quite simply. It is a wooden horse.'

'You're joking.'

'Wait and see,' answered Amos. 'The chief is a Muslim, of sorts. At least, he likes to share festivals with Muslim chiefs farther north to show his importance. There they can raise horses, where the plains are clearer and there are few mosquitoes and flies. The chiefs of the large towns ride out on horseback, with rich trappings, on special occasions. Our chief is a pagan at heart, but he wanted to join the other rulers, and he brought a succession of horses.

They all got the sleeping fever here, and died one after another. Then the agent of one of the stores had a bright idea. He found that a firm in Germany made wooden horses, life size and mounted on wheels, and he obtained one. When the chief goes on parade, he mounts the wooden horse and is pulled along by servants with ropes. If it is a long distance the horse is sent by train or lorry and the chief follows by car. I wanted to surprise you, but perhaps it is better to give you a warning, so that you don't laugh. The chief takes it very seriously.'

Our party came to a high wall, with two wooden gates. We were expected and passed through into a wide compound. In the middle was a two-storey house built of granite blocks. There was a veranda in front, with pillars at the entrance crowned by two concrete models of smirking lions.

The chief, to show respect and informality, came down the steps to meet us, and we were shown into a lounge with well-upholstered chairs. Soft drinks were served, probably on previous advice from Amos that we were, or should be, teetotal. We drank toasts and then, asking the chief about his horse, we were led to a stable in a corner of the compound.

The doors were opened and a wooden horse towered over us. It was painted chestnut brown, with bright eyes and red harness. Large wheels with solid rubber tyres were fixed to each foot. We expressed admiration and examined the animal's fine points and accurate anatomy. Sceptics may question this story, but it is simple fact, witnessed by me in 1944.

To make conversation we asked the chief, through Amos, if many Europeans visited the town of Dassa Zoumé.

'Small, small,' he replied. 'But once there were many.'

'When was that?'

'Our fathers told us that when the first white men came here they always arrived at the market early in the morning, before our people came out of their houses. They spread out their wares on the ground and sat still in the same places all day. Only when everybody had gone home did the whites pack up and leave for their camp.'

'Why did they stay so long?'

'That is what our fathers wondered,' the chief replied. 'So they planned to get to the market-place in the dark before the Europeans came. By the light of their torches they found there were holes in the ground where the white men had been sitting. Our fathers filled these holes with black warrior ants and then hid to see what would happen. When the whites arrived at dawn they sat down on the holes, and then they jumped up and ran away with the ants biting them. Our people burst out laughing, for they saw that the white men had tails. They were like monkeys!'

The chief roared with laughter. We joined in and then asked, 'Do you still believe that white men have tails?'

115

'Oh, no,' replied the chief. 'I have been in the army and travelled to France. I have seen many naked white men. Naked white women too. I have been to the Folies Bergères in Paris.'

We made our farewells and went home through the village. As we walked, the sun was setting, but it seemed to be getting dark early. There was a hush over the place, and drums started beating, while people looked at us doubtfully and went into their houses.

'There are sun spots,' exclaimed Partner. With the naked eye we could see dark patches on the disc of the sun through the evening mist.

'That could be a good omen for you,' said Amos. 'The people believe something supernatural is happening, and they may link it to your presence.'

This too occurred at that time in 1944, and we were reminded of the eclipse in the tale of *King Solomon's Mines* and the advantage it gave to the strangers in that story.

* * * * *

At Dassa the Protestant mission was to the south of the town, but the Roman Catholic mission, church, schools and houses, like an army camped opposite, lay to the north beyond the railway station. It was a larger settlement than ours, with extensive gardens and plantations for vegetables and fruit trees, and playing fields for the school children.

'Why are you anxious for us to visit the Catholics?' we asked Amos.

'I am not anxious,' he replied, 'but they are the only other white people in Dassa, a French priest and two nuns.'

'Isn't there any poaching from them, or from you, taking each other's schoolchildren?'

'There is. Father Pichon is an expert sheep or lamb-stealer, my members tell me. I suspect they are going to open a lycée, since one of the nuns is qualified in teaching. I doubt if the priest or his assistants have the proper diplomas. But he may wonder whether we are going to expand our work and start a lycée before them. The three of you should make an impression. Don't tell him why you are here.'

We set out after tea the next day, passing through the village where people looked at us respectfully, men clapping their hands and women bowing but slipping into their houses. We came to a plantation of coconut palms, with a house at each end, separated by school buildings and a church.

'I shall let you go on your own,' said Amos. 'I am going to have a talk with his catechist.'

The three of us turned right to the priest's house. We arrived at the bungalow and stood there, clapping hands in the customary manner to announce our presence. A voice called us to enter and we climbed the concrete steps, crossed a veranda, and went into a stuffy lounge. An overhead punkah was being pulled by a small boy outside the rear window tugging on a cord.

Father Pichon was of medium height and stout build, with dark hair and a straggling beard streaked with grey. He wore a grubby white cassock and was sprawled in a wicker chair. But his face lit up when he saw visitors, and he struggled to his feet.

'Enter, gentlemen. What a kindness.'

We introduced ourselves and were offered chairs.

'Ah, pioneers of the foreign mission,' said Fr Pichon. 'How good of you to visit a solitary priest in this wilderness. Have a drink.'

There were several bottles of white wine on a side table, and the priest called a boy to fetch more tumblers.

'Nothing, thank you,' said Stacey.

'Oh, but you must. I am sure you are not all teetotal.'

'This is an excellent quality,' I said.

'C'est du vin de messe' (it is Mass wine), he whispered.

'Don't you use red wine, for the symbolism of blood?' I asked.

'Oh, no,' he answered. 'White wine does not soil the altar cloths so much.'

'Then your very good health.'

'Thank you, and yours, all of you. The kindly sisters in Algeria send us this special grape juice for our tropical mission. They are more friendly than those types in the other house. Do you know, I am not allowed any authority over those nuns, and they do not come to me for confession. They are not even accountable to my bishop, and at the slightest chance they appeal to their headquarters in Rome. Fancy that, they are in the heart of Rome, getting the ear of his Holiness the Pope. Have a refill.'

'I think that's enough.'

'Une larme d'amitié' (a tear for friendship).

'Well, we want to be friends. Just a little. Do you get a good supply of this fine vintage?'

'Generally, though my bishop complains that I celebrate Mass too often! Think of it! What a reward for my zeal! But after I have finished my stock, what shall I do? It will be a crisis. Fortunately I still have a few friends in other parishes.'

We expressed sympathy and the priest inquired about our visit. We tried to give an impression of reinforcements and spoke generally of expansion. Father Pichon eyed us suspiciously and then sank back with another glass. After a second bottle had been opened we took our leave, with protestations of friendship from the lonely priest.

Amos joined us at the entrance to the compound.

'Father Pichon seems amiable enough,' I said.

'It is when he is sober that he can be most difficult,' said Amos. 'A little while ago the Commandant, the District Officer from Savalou, called on me.

We got on well, but the next morning he went to see Father Pichon, who was sober and suspicious.'

'Did he know of the visit to you?'

'Probably. The Commandant is a Catholic, of sorts, but he told the priest he thought of bringing his half-caste child to be baptized by us. He did not, of course, but he said it to annoy the priest. There was a great row and they insulted each other. The Commandant called Pichon a black crow, and the priest called him a Freemason.'

'In France that means an atheist. Are they still at war?'

'I think there is a truce now. The Commandant has been to see Pichon again for a drink, perhaps many drinks. He realizes that evening is the best time, when the priest is under the influence and more mellow.'

* * * * *

In those days, contacts between Catholics and Protestants in Dahomey were rare, confined to official functions and meetings. Relationships may be better now, after the Second Vatican Council and its openness. We found later in France, that if the priests knew we were English Protestants they welcomed us with open arms at their services.

Father Pichon was a difficult character and not popular with his colleagues. I saw him infrequently, but once, having heard that he was ill, I called at his house and left a message with his cook. The next day a French priest who was caring for him called at my Dassa bungalow and thanked me for the visit. Later in the year, after running out of quinine, I had an attack of malaria. Quinine tablets were not obtainable in Dassa village but, unknown to me, my cook went to the Catholic mission, where one of the sisters gave him some tablets from their small stock.

15. UP COUNTRY

Although Dahomey (Bénin) looks small and narrow on maps, in the central parts there were thick forests and uncultivated land. In villages, in what was called the 'bush', there were churches or chapels which needed visits, with baptisms and communions, and during 1944 I travelled widely from Dassa. Stacey and Partner had returned to the Ivory Coast, and I was formally superintendent of all Methodist Dahomey.

Travel was difficult in wartime, as petrol was tightly rationed. Amos and I walked or cycled to villages near Dassa, along bumpy or rocky footpaths. Sometimes we set out before daybreak, in the cool of early morning, greeting farm workers and stopping at fields of pineapples to help ourselves to juicy refreshment.

Petrol was saved for longer journeys, and we decided to take a western road up country as far as Pira, and then leave the van to go on foot through the forest and be met a week later on the eastern road at Kilibo. We set off early and passed through the administrative town of Savalou before dawn, thus avoiding the need to call on the government commandant. His flag was not yet hoisted, but as we passed by there came the sound of the first morning bugle.

We had a chauffeur for the mission van. I had not yet learned to drive, and one attempt on my own had nearly wrecked the car shelter. Moïse was a competent driver; he did not know much about the working of the engine, but he could change a tyre, mend a puncture or clean the carburettor.

I still remember his comments on animals we passed in villages. Sheep always seemed to cross the road when we approached.

'Mouton là,' he commented, 'faut toujours qu'il rentre chez-lui.' (Sheep, he must always go home.)

Once on a forest road a young deer burst out of the bush, gave us a scared look, and ran alongside the car for some distance before plunging into the undergrowth.

'La croose, la croose,' (the course, the race), cried Moïse. Then he reproached me for never carrying a gun. What a fine meal we had missed.

We reached Pira before noon. It was a wayside village, with a small rest-house for visitors, consisting of one room and a veranda under a thatched roof. The villagers were all out in the fields, and we waited in the rest-house till evening before meeting them in the chapel.

People were glad to see us, but when we asked for three porters the young men disappeared. We did not have a great safari, in East African style, but we needed carriers for camp-beds and cooking materials and had tried to trim down the numbers of porters needed. We could have girls, the villagers said, but we refused to give them heavy burdens and take them to strange places. It took a long time to find able and willing boys, but in the end this was arranged.

We agreed to leave before daybreak, which should bring us to the first village before morning heat. I had the only alarm clock and set it for five o'clock. I woke when it seemed to be getting light and found that the clock had stopped at twelve. But there was a clear moon and it appeared to be setting. We woke our party and went off along forest paths. But, instead of setting, the moon got brighter and we realized that it was rising. It was about one or two in the morning, but we carried on. We reached the first village long before dawn. All the huts were closed, and no one stirred. We sat down in the village square till an old woman came out to brush her path. She was full of apologies to the strangers and soon brought us coconut milk.

In the forest there were wild animals but nothing like the great herds of the East African plains; and if human beings invaded their territory, most of them kept out of the way. Sometimes we saw baboons scrambling up rocks, and once two wild cows burst out of the bush, stared at us and dashed off in another direction. In one village they told us that elephants, walking through the previous week, had pulled the thatch from the roofs of several huts. But in twenty years in West Africa, walking and driving through forests from the Ivory Coast to the Cameroons, I never saw an elephant or a lion.

There were plenty of snakes and rats, though snakes kept out of the way if possible. They did not attack, and would only turn if trodden on. In one village my camp bed had been put up in a long hut, with people at the other end. From the thatched roof hung bunches of rice, and after dusk rats, attracted by the rice, could be clearly seen. They ran about the floor of the hut all night, despite the fact that I had my evening meal early and retired to bed, tucking in the mosquito net tightly.

Another day, I was having breakfast and my boy was packing up the camp bed when a tiny creature jumped out. It was a shrew, and more than that in African humour.

'It is the elephant's mother,' cried my boy. 'Master, you are a great man. You have slept with the elephant's mother.'

Once I was sleeping in a catechist's house, but the doors were left wide open all night because of the oppressive heat. It was a lonely village, and in the evening cries could be heard in the forest from various wild animals. The villagers said that lions prowled round at times if they were hungry and might take away a wandering child. My camp bed had four struts at the corners to support the mosquito net. In the middle of the night I woke up to find the net had been pushed back and a strut seemed to be broken. Then I felt the hot sweet breath of an animal on my face, and thought of a lion. I had a torch under the pillow, pulled it out and switched it on. In the beam a young cow, which had found its way into the house, snorted and stumbled back, and then managed to get out of the doorway and run off. I shut the door, despite the heat.

* * * * *

After only a few days Amos and I came out on the eastern road at Kilibo, earlier than had been arranged with the van, and we had two adventures before its arrival.

Kilibo was a sizeable village, on the railway line from Dassa to the terminus at Parakou. But as we passed the first huts it seemed that the whole village was gathered in an open square. At one side was a large shady tree and under it sat the village chief, behind a table, flanked by several policemen in short uniforms. In front of the table stood an old woman, dressed in a single cloth and with her arms tied with rope behind her.

The chief was surprised to see us (embarrassed, we realized later), but he rose and welcomed us, getting chairs brought for Amos and myself. We saluted him, asked about his health, and the village, the crops and the weather. Then, almost casually, we asked,

'What has the old lady done?'

'She has eaten eleven people,' the chief replied. At our sceptical reaction, he listed relatives and neighbours of hers that had died, while the crowd hissed and booed.

'It doesn't seem to have done her any good,' I said. 'With eating eleven people she should be fatter.'

'She is a witch,' he asserted. 'It is their souls she has eaten. That is why she is so old, taking their soul-substance for herself.'

'We don't believe in witchcraft,' I said.

'Yes, but we Africans know it is true. You do not live like us.'

'If she has eaten people, killed them, these must be capital charges', I said, 'and tried at the district court at Parakou. I am going on to there when my van arrives.'

'You will not say anything?' he asked nervously.

'That depends on what happens to the old lady. I know the Commandant at Parakou well. Now I am tired. I must go to the church house for a rest.'

The chief shook hands profusely, wished me a comfortable stay, and whispered that the old woman would not be harmed. I knew, and he knew, that he had no right to try a murder charge, and that a French court would throw out his accusations of witchcraft.

Later that evening I received a present from the chief of a couple of chickens and a basket of yams. I heard that the old woman had been paraded round the village, then released and told not to offend again, which seemed a very light penalty for eating eleven people. But she was a lonely old person and had no relatives left to care for her.

We stayed in Kilibo two days. There was a pretty chapel, rather like a Swiss mountain church, with clay walls, whitewashed, thatched roof, and a tower, from which a single bell called children to school and members to church services. The chapel had been built in the thirties by railway workers and lay preachers, as the railway line was extended to the north. On the second evening a storm blew up, dark clouds rapidly covering the sky, thunder crackling and rain falling in torrents. As we looked out of the catechist's house we saw flames in the village.

'A house has been struck by lightning,' we cried, and rushed down to the square, getting soaked at once.

One of a row of huts was blazing fiercely, and I could see that it was joined to the next hut by a low wall which was topped with a thatch coping.

'Why doesn't somebody go and pull that thatch off, to stop the fire spreading?' I shouted.

'Oh, no,' they said, 'that is Shango' (the thunder god). 'He will strike us if we stop his work.'

I thought Shango would not bother with me, so I stepped forward and started pulling the thatch off the wall. But I was surprised that other people then came to help, and the fire was stopped from spreading.

The storm passed quickly and the fire died down, only one house being gutted. When it was quieter I told the villagers, 'You pulled down the thatch. Shango will get you.'

'Oh, no,' they said unanimously, 'you are the man.'

That was over fifty years ago, and Shango seems to have forgotten me.

* * * * *

In the villages I had to visit the churches, meet the members, and encourage the catechists in their teaching and pastoral work. Baptisms of adults and infants were held after careful examinations. Would-be church members, or

124

parents, were expected to know the Lord's Prayer, the Ten Commandments, the Apostles' Creed, and give evidence of their faith and conduct. They should be monogamous, husbands of one wife, though there was difference of opinion and practice among pastors on whether believing wives of polygamists could be baptized, and what the other women should do if only one wife was to remain.

Religious and moral teaching was done by the catechists, who were the true pastors and evangelists. On our brief visits we could only speak in generalities and often wondered how much people understood. Between Kilibo and Parakou there was a new area, where the catechist, Salomon Ogouma, had broken fresh ground. I spoke, through his interpretation, to an attentive crowd, expounding a parable; I think it was the Prodigal Son. An old lady sat in front and listened intently. At the end she said to the catechist, 'I always knew there was something like that. I have been waiting for it all my life.'

* * * * *

We went on to Parakou and I paid a courtesy call on the administrator. He was a pleasant and friendly man, and on a previous visit, since I was English and he was a Gaullist, we had talked at length about political and military changes in West Africa and Allied progress during the war in Italy. But this time he was formal, and I thought rather cold. As I was leaving his office, he called out and seized my hand.

'Ah, c'est vous. C'est la barbe.' (It is you. It's the beard.)

He had not recognized me at first, because I had been growing a beard for the last fortnight. I was tired of shaving every day and it was a nuisance, when travelling in the bush, to require hot water every morning. So I was developing quite a black beard, which changed my looks. At the railway station that afternoon I was cut dead by another acquaintance, till he too realized that the beard had changed my looks. I shaved it off that evening.

I did not tell the Commandant all that had happened at Kilibo, but I remarked that I had seen the chief at work, and wondered how detailed all his records were. The Commandant said that the chief was old and should be retired, and from the look he gave me I could see that change would be made.

* * * * *

Back at Dassa I had a long discussion with the catechists of the district about their personal situation and needs. During the war and under Vichy France, imported goods were very scarce in French West Africa. Even after the liberation and the arrival of some trade from Britain, imports were slow in arriving, and most stayed in the coastal towns and did not reach the interior.

In mid-1944 I arranged with Amos to have a break and go down to Porto Novo. A deputation of village catechists said that they were very much in need of good cloth, of various colours and textures, for women's dresses and men's suits, and they could not afford the high prices of the few rolls of material that got through to the shops. If I could buy some rolls, they would pay me coast prices on return. Most of their wives worked, with village stalls and dressmaking, and they would refund me fully.

In Porto Novo I went to see John Holt's African manager and persuaded him to let me have a dozen rolls of the best cloth, of assorted kinds for men and women, at reduced prices.

Fortunately I had come in the mission van, for there would have been too much to take on a train.

I set off on the return journey to Dassa, with my houseboy-cook, Joel, and the cloths piled in the back of the car, covered with sacking to protect them from the dust of the road. About halfway we reached the large market town of Bohicon, and Joel said to me and the chauffeur, 'Let us stop here. There is a small shelter under the trees, where you can rest and get fresh drinks.'

'A good break,' I agreed, 'but not too long. An hour at most. We want to be in Dassa before dark. We don't want to get stuck behind a dusty lorry in the night.'

We found the palm-leaf shelter and bought fresh orange drinks at a stall. Joel met a friend and excused himself, while the chauffeur and I wandered round the market, looking at medicine stalls with dried rats, dried bats, porcupine quills, herbs and grasses, as well as fruit and vegetables. There was little cloth on sale.

Joel came back and we reached Dassa at dusk, driving up the main road of the small town as tiny oil lamps began to twinkle. We ran the car into the garage and, at Joel's suggestion, decided that as we were tired and dirty the unpacking could be left until next day in the light.

In the morning there was no sign of Joel, no hot water for shaving and no breakfast prepared. I opened the shutters of the house and found the outside kitchen empty, so I made a frugal breakfast of bread and oranges. I went out to the garage and looked in the back of the van, but where there had been rolls of cloth there were now only bundles of dirty sacking and old newspapers.

The chauffeur came up from the town and catechists arrived expecting to see the cloth, but there were exclamations of dismay on hearing the news. As one man, they made for the kitchen and an adjoining room where Joel usually slept. They searched all round and in the compound outside but found no trace.

'It's that Joel,' they chorused. 'We never trusted him. He is from another tribe, from Ouidah.'

'It must have happened at Bohicon,' I said. 'He suggested a stop and, because people are usually so honest, we neither closed the van when we went round the market nor checked the cloth when we left.'

Nothing could be done, but the catechists were downcast, not only because the cloth was lost but also when they heard I had paid for it out of my own money.

Before Christmas I was going down to Porto Novo again, and the catechists came to see me.

'We want you to accept this,' said Antoine, the senior of them, holding out a large envelope.

'What is it?' I asked.

'It is the money you lost for the cloth.'

'I cannot possibly take it from you. You have had nothing.'

'Are all white men so proud?' asked Antoine. 'You paid out the money for us, and you were robbed solely on our account.'

'But you have very poor salaries.'

'We had saved, and we have friends. Our wives work, and the cloth was mostly for them. You will have the anger of the women on you if you refuse the money.'

'Very well. I will take the money in the spirit in which it was given. I can go to see John Holt's and I shall do my best to get replacements. Perhaps I can play on the conscience of their agent, after the way they exploit people, or get him to put it down to incidentals.'

This was managed, and they did not have to pay twice for their cloth. On first coming out to Africa a colleague warned me never to expect gratitude from the people. But this opinion, like many others, was false.

* * * * *

This was my last long stay in Dassa Zoumé and central Dahomey. But much later we were at the University College of Ibadan, Nigeria, and after nine years were leaving there in 1958 to take up a new appointment in London University. We decided to pay a final visit from Ibadan to Dahomey, since there were now rough but passable roads to the north. Mary, our son Stephen and I took this way to Dahomey, staying a night at Parakou and then several days at Dassa Zoumé. We met local people and visited nearby villages, and I was told that a rumour went round, 'The old lion is back.'

16. TO COURT

Now I must go back to earlier, more significant struggles in Porto Novo. The first was personal, and trying at the time. The second was fatal, and affected all our work. It seemed sometimes that our British colleagues in Nigeria, let alone at the Mission House in London, did not realize the suspicions and even hostility to which we might be subject in French-ruled Africa. Some French colonials appeared to think we had political designs on their territory, even in the church, and coolness or animosity increased as the Second World War came with its varying fortunes and divisions.

On our first married tour we had trouble on arrival with the police and the military doctor, as described earlier, and worse was to come before our departure on leave. At the end of 1937 Ernest Harrop, a teacher in the Ivory Coast, came through to Dahomey as one of the representatives for Synod. I had lived with him for a year at the Dabou seminary in 1934, where he taught in a boys' school, and so it was natural that he should stay with us in Porto Novo.

Harrop was feverish when he arrived and was sent to bed. But he called me to his room. 'I am in great pain,' he said, 'and I have this.'

He pulled down his shorts and showed a swelling in his groin, as big as a hen's egg.

'What's that?' I asked.

'I don't know. It has just come up. It was quite small when I left Dabou, but now it is hurting and getting bigger.'

Mary was a nurse and examined him. We decided he must be taken to the hospital, for professional advice, if not care. We took him to the military hospital in Porto Novo, where he was seen by a medical orderly.

'The doctor is away visiting the army in the interior,' he said. 'Can I help?'

'I don't know,' replied Ernest. 'Would you kindly examine me?'

He stripped and lay down on a hard flat couch covered with shiny cloth. The orderly looked at the swelling, prodded it, while Ernest winced, and fetched iodine to paint it.

'You say you live in the bush in the Ivory Coast,' she asked. 'Are there many rats about?'

'It isn't really bush or forest but a large clearing in open savanna country. The house where I live is built of granite and concrete and is always clean. Why do you ask?'

'I know that swellings like this may be buboes, caused by plague carried by rats.'

'Plague? But surely there would be an epidemic? I have heard nothing of any similar illness in the village.'

'I say, that is all I know. Anyway, we can do no more for you at the moment. Go home. Stay in bed. Take quinine and aspirin. Perhaps the doctor will visit you when he returns.'

We went back to the seminary dissatisfied and worried.

'What about the Dabou rats?' I asked.

'They are bush rodents,' Harrop answered. 'Nothing to do with dirt and refuse, I am sure. The natives eat them. You remember them?'

I did indeed. The two-storey seminary house at Dabou had an outside wooden staircase leading to bedrooms along a wooden-floored corridor. Rats came there, I recalled vividly. They crept in from the savanna grasses at night and could be heard jumping up from stair to stair of the house. We bought large steel traps to catch them, but some were caught half-alive in the traps and they jumped up or down the stairs dragging the metal traps with them. Other rats were killed, but the survivors would never touch the fatal traps again, however much they were washed.

These rats gave me nightmares. In my sleep I heard them jumping up the wooden staircase and scuttling along the corridor. The noise of scratching stopped outside my bedroom door, but then an invisible hand seemed to turn the door knob, as visitors turned it during the day. I awoke in a cold sweat. Eventually we got rid of most of the rats by buying two large cats.

Harrop's pains and fever got worse, and after three days action became imperative.

'That doctor has never come,' he said. 'In any case, he's a soldier and probably knows little more than his orderly. I don't believe this is plague. But can't you get me to a better hospital?'

'Cotonou hospital is not much better than this one,' I replied. 'There is Lagos, they have a large hospital, but there's no launch till next week. I've been making inquiries. The only hope is John Holt's. They might have one of their own lighters going along the lagoon.'

This was arranged. There was a lighter nearly full of palm oil, and John Holt's agent agreed to send it off to Lagos at once, and allowed us to travel on board.

* * * * *

The lighter was a long barge, almost all cargo, with the hold covered by tarpaulins over planks. It chugged gently along the lagoon and passed the frontiers before dark, with stamping of papers and cursory examination of the hold at the two hulks. Nothing was said about Harrop's illness, and he received hardly a glance from the clerks as he lay stretched out on a camp bed. Mary and I had deck chairs beside him, and apart from four mechanics we were alone and enjoyed the quiet.

In the evening we anchored at Badagry, and the two of us got off and sat in the moonlight for a while on the steps of an old rest house, while Harrop stayed on board the lighter. Then we carried on through the night and into the heat of next morning. We went very slowly, and it was afternoon when the lighter tied up at a small wharf in Lagos.

We called a taxi, and Harrop was taken straight to the large town hospital and admitted after some delay. Mary and I went to the boys' high school and were given hospitality. We said nothing about the suggestion of plague.

Next morning we went to the hospital and found that Harrop, had been some time in casualty, before being transferred to a medical ward and examined by a European doctor. After a long wait the doctor received us.

'Plague?' he said, in response to our query. 'That would be most dangerous, and I would have to put you all in quarantine. But no, that's nonsense. Your friend is completely exhausted, and he needs more than any medicines we can give him here. He has swellings in other glands. It is general debility, added to a vicious malaria which brings on further symptoms and could cause complete collapse. The only cure, if there is one, would be a change of air. He should return to Europe at once.'

'Will he get better?'

'I am sorry to be brutal,' the doctor replied, 'but I see you are facing possibilities. If this country is no longer the white man's grave, neither is it a health resort. There are mysterious and fatal sicknesses. I cannot answer your question positively. Your friend must leave at once and get away from the tropics. But there is always hope that sea air and eventual hospitalization in England may save him. If he can get there.'

'What must we do?'

'Send him home immediately. An Elder Dempster ship leaves Lagos every week. The *Apapa* is in. It's not a Cunard liner, but get him on it, or I won't answer for the consequences.'

The ship passage was arranged with the mission secretary. We saw Harrop on board, and as we were leaving we heard one sailor say to another, 'He won't get there. Another burial at sea.'

Fortunately, he did survive the journey and, after treatment at the hospital for tropical diseases and home leave, he returned to the Ivory Coast.

* * * * *

Mary and I went back to Porto Novo on the regular German launch, returning to the heat and mosquitoes of that town under the swastika flag.

But we settled into the routine, with the hope of our own furlough in a few months.

One afternoon we were resting in siesta when there was clapping outside. I looked down through the shutters on the garden below and called, 'What is it?'

'Police'

'What, again?'

'A notice for you, sir.'

I went downstairs and saw the friendly sergeant. He saluted with respect, but handed over a formal buff envelope with writing in purple ink. I opened it and exclaimed, 'But this is a summons!'

'I am sorry, sir.'

'What is it for? It doesn't say.'

'I cannot tell, sir. It has come from the court office in Cotonou.'

'All it says is that we must appear, my wife and I, at the court to answer charges.'

I climbed the stairs and hesitated before going in to Mary. How could the news be broken to her? It could not be hidden, since she must appear with me at the court. And she called out cheerfully, 'What was it? Your grandmother's aunt's maiden name?'

'Take it easy, old girl. Don't get alarmed. It's from the court.'

'What court?'

'Cotonou. We have to appear there. To answer charges, unspecified.'

'There's always something bad here,' she cried. 'Just when it seemed things were going better those dreadful police come again. And the court? Why should we go? We haven't done anything wrong.'

'We must get advice. I know, I'll ask Jacques Viéville at the treasury.'

I went to see Viéville, and a few days later he called me to his office.

'Have you had trouble with the doctor?' he asked.

'Last year, when we first arrived.'

'This is more recent. You were in Lagos a week or two ago, I believe.'

'Yes, but there were no restrictions when we came back.'

'Are you sure? I would advise you to get any witnesses you can of your departure and return, from your colleagues or friends or employees, especially your chauffeur or anyone who met you when you came back. This doctor has laid charges against you for ignoring his instructions. He is unpopular, and boosts his ego by taking revenge for opposition among Europeans and Africans by persecuting anybody he can get at. Besides, you are English, and Protestant. He is a narrow-minded Anglophobe and formally Catholic.'

I talked to other people in the mission and government, trying to get advice as to the best course of action, and was not happy with the results.

'What gets me', I confided to Suzanne Marlier at the girls' school one day, 'is that people seem to assume we have done wrong. Is this the French way of treating you as guilty until you are proved innocent? People imagine we must have disregarded health regulations or offended the doctor, unpopular though he is, or broken the law in some other way. So-called 'friends' suppose they are helping by saying that for a breach of the health regulations the maximum penalty is a fine of several thousand francs or six months in prison, but the jail sentence is not often passed on whites.'

'Job's comforters,' she said. 'But did you know that the doctor came to the seminary after you had taken Monsieur Harrop to Lagos?'

'No, I did not. Nobody told me.'

'I was not there myself,' she said, 'and I have only just heard of it. Your house was empty, of course, and the students were on holiday. There was

134

only the watchman, that Kiti, and his version was garbled because his French is so sketchy. But he told my gardener that the doctor arrived at last, as you had requested, to see Monsieur Harrop, and he found you had all gone. He tried to get some information and went away angry. He must have made other inquiries to discover that you had left for Lagos. You went on a John Holt's barge and came back on the regular launch, I think?'

'Yes. Oh dear! The doctor probably had a grudge against us from our first encounter, and it sounds as if he would be angry because Ernest Harrop had been taken to Nigeria. There might be professional or nationalistic jealousy. And a suspicion of plague suggested by his orderly would make matters worse.'

'Maybe, though, that army doctor would not be competent himself to deal with a very serious illness, and he could hardly blame you for seeking better treatment than you could get here.'

'If we had done it with his help. But he was not there. We were caught between alternatives, but that might not stop him launching a vendetta against us. He cannot get at Harrop now, but we are at his mercy, or the court's.'

* * * * *

In due course we presented ourselves at the court at Cotonou. A formal note was taken of our names, residence and occupations, and the charge of being in flagrant breach of health regulations on entering the colony of Dahomey was indicated. A trial date was fixed for two months later, and we were allowed to go back home to Porto Novo without bail, but ordered to present ourselves again on the prescribed day.

We were due to go on leave in May, and a passage was tentatively booked for us on a French ship direct from Cotonou to France, which seemed more sure than going by launch to Lagos for a British ship there. Mary's condition, which required leave before June, was a source of some anxiety. But everything depended on the outcome of the trial.

135

When the time came, we appeared at the court house in Cotonou, a long low building in the centre of town, with tiled floors and whitewashed walls. The doors and windows were open to air from the sea, but there was a haze and little freshness. Punkahs were pulled from the ceiling by khaki-clad prisoners sitting against the walls of the rooms. There were crowds of people, squatting on the sandy ground outside the court and crushing into doorways whenever an interesting name was called.

We arrived early and were given chairs at the back of the major court room but were not called all morning. After a break for lunch, and a short siesta, the court resumed at three o'clock and our case was the last of the day.

A lightly-coloured Martiniquan magistrate sat at a table on a raised platform, with two African clerks at lower tables and an interpreter beside them. Mary and I were called to stand in front of the magistrate, and he ordered a chair to be provided for the lady, as she was clearly pregnant. The interpreter was told to act for her, if her French proved inadequate for answering all the questions.

'This is a case', the magistrate began, 'to answer a charge laid by the medical officer in Porto Novo. He complains that you, Madame, and you, Monsieur, have come into this country fragrantly and repeatedly ignoring the instructions which he had issued for the protection of the health of the colony, and disobeying his orders through his officers. This is serious. I have consulted the Gazette. Have you any witnesses?'

'Our chauffeur was at the wharf when we last arrived,' I said, 'and he is here with us.'

'There is an officer from the doctor,' said the magistrate. 'We will hear them both.'

The court heard the doctor's orderly swear on oath that he had both approached and warned Mary and me of the health restrictions on our last entry into the country from Nigeria, and of a requirement to report to the hospital, which had been disobeyed.

Then Joseph, our chauffeur, swore the opposite. He had waited at the wharf for two hours, he said, because the launch was late. No orderly had appeared or spoken to him or addressed us. He knew the orderly, he said, with a smile.

Then I told the court of our first arrival in Porto Novo sixteen months ago, of the confusion over restrictions, and our efforts to set things right. I described Harrop's illness, the essential journey to the hospital in Lagos in the doctor's absence, and Harrop's return to Europe. I affirmed that when we came back we were not advised or challenged by any health officer.

Mary repeated this in English, to which the magistrate listened closely, since he appeared to understand it, though it was translated into French by the interpreter. The magistrate shuffled through his papers and we waited fearfully until he gave judgement.

'This is a clear case of persecution,' he began, and we relaxed. 'You are not visitors to Dahomey, but residents of Porto Novo. Therefore you did not come into the country, as the charge maintains, on the last occasion, which is the only one in question. The Catholic fathers are always slipping over the border to visit their flock in Nigeria, but I have not heard of them being challenged or charged on their return. The two witnesses cancel each other out, with a possibility of perjury which could be referred to the public prosecutor.'

'Your own accounts are consistent,' he continued. 'I credit you, Madame, and you, Monsieur, with truthful testimony. You would have taken care to obey regulations, if they were in force, after your first experiences with this doctor and with the police, of which you have told me and which I find instructive. Most important, there is no evidence of Yellow Fever orders being in force, apart from a letter from the doctor. Health restrictions should be printed in the weekly official Gazette, and I have not found such for the week in question. There is also a mention of plague, though it appears from your evidence that it was not plague. In any case it is irrelevant to this charge, which is that of flouting rules against Yellow Fever when entering the country. I find the charge not proved.'

'Does that mean we can go?' I asked.

'Of course,' the magistrate replied. 'You are not guilty. You are free.'

'Hurrah for French justice!' we exclaimed as we embraced outside the court.

137

'I always knew you would get off, sir,' said Joseph, the chauffeur.

'Thank you for your help, Joseph,' I answered. 'You had more faith in us than some of our white friends.'

* * * * *

So in May we went home on the longed for furlough. Joseph took us to Cotonou, and from the small wharf we saw a large ship of the Chargeurs Réunis line lying at anchor out to sea. As we waited on the quay to be taken off in canoes the sea was choppy, and at the coast long rollers broke loudly on the sands. Eventually we got into a mammy-chair and were hoisted by crane into the air, and then we dangled until the waiting canoe was in the trough of a wave and we were lowered with a bump. Mary went pale in the rough seas and clasped her hand over her mouth to stop being sick.

The rowers sang as they tried to dig their oars in time into the waves and the canoe rolled from side to side. When we reached the ship, it towered so high above us that it seemed impossible we would ever get aboard. A chain with a hook rattled down, missed us twice, and then was fastened to the top iron rail of the chair. We were heaved up, hung in the air, and then slowly lowered on to the deck of the ship. A large French stewardess looked at Mary appraisingly and took her to our cabin with care.

The origin of the term 'mammy-chair' is said by the dictionary to be 'obscure', but the French West African liners could be called 'mammy-ships'. On our ship there were others, wives of French colonials, who were largely pregnant and trying to get to France in time.

Our firstborn arrived safely at the end of June.

17. MARTYR FOR TRUTH

Our next tour at Porto Novo passed peacefully and without incident, and we began to feel at home with Dahomey and its people. But in the outside world political affairs were tense and the Second World War broke out in September 1939. Britain and France were allies again, but the future was uncertain and was to prove disastrous.

One day in the spring of 1940 we were taking tea, and cool orange squash, in the upstairs lounge of the seminary staff house. The doors and windows were wide open, front and back, and a slight breeze came in from the garden. Through the distant gate came a long black car flying the tricolour.

'Hallo,' I said. 'Not more trouble?'

The car pulled up outside our house and, seeing me on the veranda, the African driver got out, opened the rear car door and ushered the occupant up the stairs. He was a short Frenchman, with domed bald head, loose shirt, baggy shorts and sandals. He came running up and held out his hand.

'Dunglas, Edouard,' he said. 'You are the professor in charge here? And you are English?'

'Yes,' I replied.

'I am the administrator of the suburbs, and I come to ask a favour.'

'What can I do?'

'Have you a Bible?'

'Naturally, in a Protestant mission.'

'Ah, you see,' he said, 'I am a Catholic, and I have no Bible. But have you both French and English Bibles?'

'Yes,' I answered, half wondering if he was trying to catch me out for using English in a French colony.

'Then perhaps you can help me,' Monsieur Dunglas continued. 'I am an amateur of music. I have a large collection of gramophone records. You must come to my house and hear them. And Madame, of course,' he said, bowing to Mary.

'I have been in John Holt's store,' he went on. 'They have a new stock of records. They had a set of the *Messiah,* by Handel. You know it, naturally? In France it is not known. I bought the set and I have been playing it through. C'est magnifique. But there is my trouble. The words of *Messiah* are in English, and I have not adequate knowledge of your beautiful tongue to understand the words of the Bible when they are sung. Yet I am an Anglophile. Although I come from the south of France, from the Pyrenees, I have always believed in the Entente Cordiale between our two countries. And now we are allies again in this war. But what can I do, Monsieur le Pasteur, to hear and understand the words of the great *Messiah* of Handel?'

'You need a French version of the texts?' I asked.

'Precisely,' he replied. 'What is required is for some knowledgeable and well-disposed person to go through the music of *Messiah*, locate the words in the English Bible, and then they can be found for me in the French Bible. I assume that the two translations agree in chapter and verse? I can easily get my secretary to copy out the passages from a French Bible, if you would kindly sell me a copy. But what is needed first is the identification and notation of chapter and verse in English. Could you, and would you, undertake such a task?'

'I regret, Monsieur Dunglas,' I answered, 'but that is not possible. My wife and I are on the point of going on furlough to Europe. We are leaving for Lagos by the new launch.'

'I congratulate you. But, alas, what shall I do?'

'I think my colleague, Monsieur Taylor, might help you. He is taking over as principal of the seminary while I am away. Besides, he is more knowledgeable in music than I am, and he knows the Bible well.'

'Where can I find this amiable gentleman?'

'He lives in a flat over the seminary. I will take you to see him.'

Monsieur Dunglas trotted along beside me to the seminary flat, and arrangements were soon fixed up with Taylor.

'You've landed me with a fine long task,' he said after Dunglas had gone.

'You will make a friend while we are away,' I told him. 'A contact like that in the administration is always useful.'

These words might have been prophetic, but they were ominous.

* * * * *

Ernest Taylor arrived in Porto Novo in the autumn of 1939. He was an important addition to our staff, a good scholar and teacher, and a promising future was predicted for him in the church and beyond.

Ernest had been trained at Headingley College, Leeds, and before going there had prepared himself by taking a London Bachelor of Arts degree. At Headingley he was told to follow the normal three year course for the London Bachelor of Divinity, but he knew that he could be exempted from part of it through his first degree and he could complete the study required in two years. He did this, entered for the examination privately, and gained an honours degree as an external student, as I did also. His college tutors were astonished.

'What is this, Mr Taylor?' asked the Principal. 'I see from the list that you have obtained the BD already, and with honours.'

'Yes, sir.'

'But after only two years?'

'I thought it would be useful, and save repetition.'

'But you have a three year course here. You must complete the period required by our regulations. What will you do in your third year?'

'If I must stay,' replied Taylor, 'it would be helpful to prepare myself for overseas work by further study. You know that I have been designated for French West Africa and, if I can, I should like to attend an advanced French course in Leeds university, and perhaps another also in anthropology.'

'I see. It is most irregular. But I will have a word with the university authorities.'

Ernest told us all this later in Porto Novo, and we admired his perseverance and the fluency that he had gained in French language and literature, as well as studying anthropology and the religions of African peoples, which was a vast area that we both felt needed research.

Ernest had come to fill the gap caused by the resignation of another English tutor in the seminary, and to provide coverage during my own absence on leave, which in the event was greatly extended through public breach of communications. His father was a baker and Ernest had helped him at times, and so he was useful to Mary in making a Christmas cake. The weather was hot and dry in December, and we ate the cake sitting outside our house in Porto Novo in the brilliant moonlight.

Ernest Taylor

War was declared against Germany on 3rd September 1939, but for a time life in Dahomey, which was under the colonial rule of France, was little affected. Some trenches were dug on the outskirts of Porto Novo town, but at that time nobody knew where the enemy might come from. There had been German agencies in shipping lines but, by contrast with the First World War, Germany had no African territory.

Britain and France were allies against Germany, and there was some improvement in relationships. The Protestant mission, to show loyalty, had always sent representatives to ceremonies at the Porto Novo war memorial on French national holidays, Bastille Day on 14th July and Armistice Day on 11th November. But after the declaration of war, Mary and I, as representatives of the British mission, were invited for the first time to dinner at the Governor's palace, a small yellowish-pink building on a rise overlooking the lagoon. The Governor and his wife were friendly, and the food and French wines were excellent.

A small weekly newspaper, *France-Dahomey,* carried what little news there was of the war, and some people had wireless sets and passed on more details. The Hôtel Bayol, a two-storey building which was all that Porto Novo could manage for public accommodation, advertized a film with the title, *Sommes-nous défendus?* (Are we defended?) Using pictures of the Maginot Line, it showed that France was impregnable, to the comfort of the local colonials.

* * * * *

In May 1940, as international events began to move, Mary and I went on furlough. We had, rightly as it turned out, thought it better to travel via Nigeria. Had we gone through France we might have been caught up as refugees in the chaos of the German invasion, or even taken prisoner. We sailed on an Elder Dempster ship from Lagos and were told to carry lifebelts at all times, while blackout was enforced on deck at nights and outside smoking forbidden. From Freetown we went in company with two other ships, and each carried a small deck gun but no other protection. The journey was rapid and peaceful, but daily radio bulletins on the ship gave alarming news of unprovoked German invasions of the Low Countries and of the breakthrough into France at Sedan. We landed safely in Liverpool and got home to the Midlands before the Dunkirk evacuation and the air raids on London. Our second child was born in July.

It is important to note some wartime events which affected our people in Dahomey. The French armistice with Germany on 21st June 1940 and the division of France into German-occupied territory and a semi-independent zone governed from Vichy brought French West Africa under Vichy control and influenced its activities.

By the terms of the German armistice the French fleet was to remain in the hands of Vichy, but the British government saw great danger there. On 3 July the British Mediterranean fleet from Gibraltar surrounded the largest concentration of French warships at Mers el-Kebir near Oran in Algeria and gave it five alternatives: joining Britain, surrendering to British crews, demilitarizing the ships, scuttling them, or sailing to the French West Indies to be disarmed.

When the French refused all these offers, their fleet was bombarded for five minutes, several battle cruisers and other ships were destroyed and 1200 French sailors were killed.

Vichy France broke off diplomatic relations with Britain, and I could not return to Dahomey for three years. Ernest Taylor found himself in charge of the Porto Novo seminary and with nominal responsibility for the whole mission and church in the country.

Bitter anti-British feeling was aroused among Vichy supporters, in France and in Africa, and even Allied sympathizers spoke of 'the tragedy of Mers el-Kebir'. In French West Africa the churches were ordered to hold memorial services for the fallen French sailors. Ernest Taylor conducted this service at Porto Novo in Ouézoumé church, in the presence of government officials. He managed this, I was told later, by combining the liturgy of morning worship with funeral prayers.

In September 1940 British and Free French forces tried to seize the port of Dakar in Senegal, so as to bring French West Africa over to the Allied side. But to their surprise the Dakar authorities refused to leave Vichy for the Gaullists and opened fire on the British fleet, hitting two warships. The action was called off, with the result that all French West Africa, including the Ivory Coast and Dahomey, remained under Vichy until late 1942. However, at the end of October 1940 French Equatorial Africa, farther down the African coast, rallied to the Free French movement, and General de Gaulle called from there on all the people in French territories to support him.

For the rest of 1940 and into 1941, Ernest Taylor had the difficult and dangerous task, as an English missionary, young and fairly new to Dahomey, under a Vichy-ruled government, of providing a steady and continuing Christian development. But the churches were calm and supportive, African ministers, catechists and members continued and even extended their work, and some said later that they had never believed in a German victory.

Most French missionaries had been conscripted into the army and, after the fall of France, they did not return to Dahomey. However, some help arrived when Paul Wood, an elderly French Methodist, and his wife managed to come out from France to provide assistance in Porto Novo. Wood, one of the missionaries recruited by W. J. Platt in 1921, had worked in the Ivory Coast before returning to churches in France. Now in middle age he came to the Porto Novo seminary to try to relieve Taylor's load of teaching, but his attitude caused some difficulties.

Wood was a fairly simple French minister, perhaps not quite fundamentalist but traditional and obstinate. He saw Africans as children and seemed to think that all that the ministers and catechists in training needed was the whole Bible, which meant its literal history and teaching. Taylor, by contrast, gave critical and historical studies of the texts of the Bible, aroused great interest among his students and remarked that, as adults in the modern world, they read newspapers and books from France. Wood confronted him,

'I teach the word of God literally,' he insisted.

'That isn't honest,' was Taylor's reply.

The following Sunday, Taylor conducted the evening service in the seminary chapel, to which other people came from schools and the town. He preached on a text from Proverbs 23:23, 'Acquiers la vérité et ne la vends pas.' (Gain the truth, and sell it not.)

The Demoiselles from the girls' school, and some others, were moved by the force and conviction of Taylor's arguments and said he looked like a prophet, or martyr, they added later. Paul Wood was not pleased, though he was impressed and long remembered it.

* * * * *

So 1940 passed, and in the new year it looked as if Ernest Taylor and the church and seminary could survive under Vichy. But in mid-1941 disaster struck.

On Whitsunday Taylor went as part of his oversight of the churches to conduct morning service in the principal Methodist church in Cotonou. There was a large congregation, and it was a long service, including adult and infant baptisms, which were traditional at Pentecost. As the crowd left the church, two French sailors joined them and made their way towards Taylor. It appeared later that they had left a ship at Cotonou pier and wanted to join the Free French forces. Perhaps they thought that Dahomey was part of Gaullist Equatorial Africa. But they found to their surprise that the country was under the rule of Vichy, and they made some imprudent inquiries. Somebody then told them that there was an Englishman at the Protestant church and they went to find him.

It has not been possible to discover precisely what Taylor said to these sailors. Some accused him of encouraging the enemies of France (his own countrymen), while Paul Wood later denied that he had said anything at all. Suzanne Marlier then muttered to me, 'I expect he told them to follow the coast road to Nigeria.' Coming from Alsace, she would have done this herself.

From the Vichy government point of view, not only should Taylor not have advised the sailors, but he should have reported their presence and actions to the police.

Whatever was or was not said, Taylor would have been prudent in view of the uncertain position of an Englishman in a French colony under Vichy and his responsibility for the churches. But the two sailors foolishly took the main road towards Nigeria, arrived at a frontier post, and were duly arrested by French guards and charged with desertion. During questioning at the police station, they were put under pressure to state who had advised them about the route they had taken in a strange country, and they mentioned the Protestant pastor.

That was enough, and on his return to the seminary in Porto Novo Ernest was met by police and soldiers, arrested and taken to the police station. There the harsh Corsican commander could hardly contain his anger and delight at seizing this enemy of Napoleon. He raved about perfidious Albion, foe of France, treason and punishment. He wanted to keep Ernest in prison and in irons, but he was told by his superiors that the matter was too grave to be dealt with locally. The prisoner must be sent to the highest court of French West Africa at Dakar in Senegal, over a thousand miles away.

146

Ernest met the accusations with firmness and dignity. When he could get a word in, he insisted that he was in charge of the Protestant mission, which was independent of political matters. If he was to be sent away, he must put the church and seminary affairs in order and hand them over to Pastor Wood, a French citizen. After refusal and bluster, and under pressure from colleagues, the Corsican police officer at last allowed the request, under strict conditions.

Monsieur Taylor must give his solemn word, his parole, that he would surrender himself to the police again next morning and must submit to being sent to Dakar. This was agreed, Ernest gave his word and was allowed home under escort and left in peace for the night.

Then there was great distress at the seminary for the Woods and the Demoiselles, and there was alarm in the church. But Ernest, pale and tired, held to his word and worked till dawn, putting his papers together for Paul Wood.

In the middle of the night there came a gentle knock at his door and it opened quietly. It was Philippe Dovoedo, the African minister at Ouézoumé church.

'You must get away to Nigeria,' he told Ernest.

'How can I do that?'

'I can guide you, with a friend who knows the way. There are paths through the bush and canoes at the swamps. I have an African robe here to disguise you, and we can blacken your face and hands. If we leave now, before dawn you will be safely over the frontier at Badagry.'

'Thank you for your thought and kindness,' said Ernest, 'but I cannot go. I have given my parole.'

'Parole? What is this thing parole?' protested Dovoedo. 'You owe it to yourself and us, to save yourself. They will kill you.'

'I think not, at least I hope not. But it is my duty, and I shall keep my word.'

Later Philipe Dovoedo told me of this conversation and what followed.

It has often been debated whether Ernest should have gone with him. He had given his word, but a parole which had been forced from him could be regarded as invalid. If he had got safely to Nigeria, he would probably be alive today, having rendered a lifetime of service to his church and country. But if he had broken his word, his colleagues could have suffered, the Woods and even the Demoiselles arrested or returned to Vichy France. The seminary and the church, or all the churches having British connections, might have been closed down as centres of disloyalty in the unease and panic of those days.

Vichy France had forced changes upon the French West African colonies, and it was the worst time of the war. Fear of triumphant Germany was everywhere. When Jean Faure, of the Paris evangelical mission in Togo, spoke out against the deportation of a Jew, he was arrested and sent back to France. Many French administrators saw the future of their country in alliance with victorious Germany, despite its declared aim of making France pay for the First World War defeat and the Treaty of Versailles. It was clear to them that Britain had lost this war. The news bulletins were full of accounts of the bombing of British cities, and no doubt Churchill would soon sue for peace. After Mers-el-Kebir the *entente cordiale* changed, for some, into hatred for Britain as *l'ennemi héréditaire*, the hereditary enemy of France.

French colonials were divided. Those loyal to Vichy were stationed in the coastal administrative towns of Porto Novo, Cotonou and Lomé, while those suspected of Allied sympathies were sent up country, out of the way. Edouard Dunglas was one of the most outspoken and had boasted openly in April 1941, 'We don't get the full news here. But I heard this morning that Admiral Cunningham has sunk the Italian fleet.'

He was referring to the battle of Matapan, at which the Italians lost cruisers, destroyers and many lives, while British casualties were slight. When Dunglas was asked how he got this news, he said that he rang through to Nigeria for information every morning. The telephone line was erratic at the best of times, but although French and British territories were supposed to have broken off relations, the inter-colonial line was still open. Dunglas was sent packing to Savalou in the interior.

If there had been support for Taylor in the administration at Porto Novo, his offence, if such it was, would have been quietly shelved or he would have been deported to Nigeria. But Jacques Viéville had gone home to France and was in the occupied zone, Dunglas was at Savalou, and others preferred to say nothing. The new Governor of the colony of Dahomey, an ardent Vichy supporter, signed the order for Taylor's despatch as a prisoner to Dakar. Three years later, after the change of regime, he sent me a cheque for the mission finances. I wondered whether I was right to deprive the church of funds, but I refused to cash it, as blood money.

After the war, this Governor was tried for wartime collaboration with Germany, given a heavy fine, and stripped of his French citizenship.

Ernest Taylor journeyed by train and lorry north and west to Dakar, under guard and sometimes handcuffed. It was a long and painful expedition. After leaving the railhead at Parakou, a convoy went up to the river Niger and then across the western Soudan and desert, avoiding British-ruled Gold Coast and Sierra Leone. Conditions were harsh and primitive, food short or tainted, water scarce, guards rough or careless. Ernest, despite his youth and strong appearance, was subject to fevers and stricken with dysentery. He was very sickly when he got to Dakar and was put in prison with criminals.

Eventually he was brought to trial and convicted of treason against the state. At the end of 1941, he was sentenced to five years imprisonment and a fine of twenty thousand francs, to be followed by expulsion from French territory. On 17th April 1942 Ernest Taylor died in prison at Dakar, and was buried by a French Reformed minister who had visited him in jail. At the end of that year, Allied armies landed in French North Africa, bringing French West Africa over to the Allied side and had Ernest lived he would have been freed and released from all charges.

The news of his death shook the church and the town of Porto Novo, and it was followed by the suicide of the King of the Night, suspected by the French colonial government of contacts with enemy Nigeria.

The church and seminary were desolated, but they carried on till the arrival of Allied troops and communications changed the political situation and direct contact with Britain was again possible. At the suggestion of the Woods, the Demoiselles and the local church, the words inscribed on Ernest Taylor's grave in Dakar were: 'Gain the truth, and sell it not.'

18. NEW DIRECTIONS

The death of Ernest Taylor affected people in Africa and Britain. When in 1940, because of the breakdown of diplomatic relations with France, our return to West Africa had become impossible, I had been sent to church work in Cornwall. As a minister, I was not liable for military service. Public notices appeared requiring all young men to register, but those exempted were regular soldiers, ministers of religion, and the insane.

In 1941 news came through to the Mission House in London of Taylor's arrest and eventual imprisonment, but it was with great shock that we heard at May Synod in 1942 of his death in Dakar the previous month. We mourned the unexpected loss of a colleague and friend, and thought of the needs of teaching and pastoral work in Dahomey, but for the moment nothing could be done.

Then, in November 1942, Allied military landings in French North Africa changed the situation completely. Rule from Vichy was broken (Germany took over the whole of France), communications were opened between Britain and the rest of Africa, and Allied troops began making roads from Senegal right along the west coast of Africa, to connect with air links to the eastern Sudan and Egypt. In French-ruled territory positions were reversed: supporters of former Vichy were relegated to country stations and Gaullists took over most of the coastal centres of government.

I soon received an anticipated inquiry from the Mission House in London. Information had been received of desperate conditions in Dahomey. Old Paul Wood at the seminary in Porto Novo needed urgently to go on long-overdue leave, and there was no other white male missionary for the whole of Dahomey. Could I, would I, go back to take over both the college teaching and the supervision of an entire country's Protestant work? It was a hard decision, since I needed to consider the safety of my wife and two young children in the war which had not yet ended, as well as housing and education.

Although Cornwall had seemed fairly safe from the blitz, in April 1941 a stray German bomber, going back to occupied France from the air over south Wales, had dropped some of his remaining load on Redruth, where we lived, and we had nearly been killed. People died on the railway station in front of us and in a house behind ours. Another foot or two in the trajectory of the bombs and we would have been destroyed and our children made orphans or wounded or killed with us. As it was, our windows and front door were blown in and ceilings collapsed, but we were all personally untouched and for some time were given a home by a kindly country lady.

Two years later, living quietly in a Cornish village, Mary and I agreed that I should return to Africa, and we hoped that she and the children might join me later. The hope kept us going, though in the event it was not realized, and I was in West Africa on my own for two and a half years. The family went to the grandparents' farm in the Midlands, the children to the village school and Mary to work in Northampton Hospital.

The return to Africa in September 1943 in a large convoy of ships has been described briefly earlier in this book. The war was far from over but most people seemed hardly to consider the dangers of sea travel, taking a stoical attitude, carrying life jackets all the time and observing the blackout at night. After changing ships at Freetown, we went on to Lagos, and then by a Nigerian launch to Porto Novo. French government officials were noticeably more friendly to the British, since we were allies again and preparing for the liberation of France.

Arrived at the seminary, I had the first task of getting Taylor's belongings into order. They were almost as he had left them two years before and needed to be sorted out, packed, crated and returned to his parents in Croydon.

Taylor had been a methodical worker and among his effects was the will which he had prudently made before going to Africa and updated in the night when he was on parole before being taken away to Dakar. To my surprise I found that he had left me some of his books, and this reminder of his friendship was a valuable legacy, since it pointed to wider concerns.

The customs and religion of Dahomey were all around us, though few foreigners took serious interest in them. But Ernest Taylor, from the days when as a student he was designated for Africa, had determined to study Dahomean religion. As far as I know, he had not written down any of the results of his research, and probably teaching and administrative duties left him no time to do so, but some of the dozen books he left me in his will aided the development of what he had begun.

Taylor had read some of the classics of traditional anthropology and some recent studies. I still have his two volumes of a Victorian work, *Primitive Culture* by E. B. Tylor, with his small neat signature and the inscription 'Headingley 1936'. Then, before going to Africa, he had bought two large volumes on Dahomey, which had just been published by an American anthropologist, Melville Herskovits. These, also, I still possess, with Ernest's signature and the note 'Croydon 1939'.

* * * * *

My own interest in what I have termed 'African Traditional Religion' had begun earlier, and I had read specialist books by African, European and American writers. Indeed, my first printed article, entitled 'The Christian Attitude to Non-Christian Religions', appeared in *The Expository Times* in 1939. It was a response to a book which had been prepared for a conference of the International Missionary Council, meeting in Madras. I was travelling back to Africa in 1938 – on my own, since Mary was staying at home for a while with our first child – and I read the book, Hendrik Kraemer's *The Christian Message in a non-Christian World,* on the boat. It was a dogmatic attack on liberal Christianity and on other world religions. The latter were accused of being 'naturalist religions of trans-empirical realization', a cryptic phrase which appeared to mean that all non-Christian religions were purely human inventions by which men tried to save themselves, pulling themselves up by their own bootlaces. Christianity, it was asserted, was antagonistic to all other 'human aspirations and ends', and could have no dealing with any other faith.

I was so angry with such narrow missionary propaganda, condemning all other religions, that I sketched a reply, writing in my cabin. I was not alone in rejecting Kraemer's book and learned later that a renowned missionary to India, C. F. Andrews, friend of Gandhi and Tagore, had 'unceremoniously dumped' his copy of Kraemer in a waste paper basket.

Great historical and scriptural religions, Hinduism, Buddhism, Islam and others, had been widely studied by European and American scholars, and

152

while in early times such religions had often been criticized or misrepresented, more recently there had come fair and objective portrayal and appreciation of many teachings and practices. But African religion had not received similar attention. It was commonly dismissed as 'heathen', 'fetish', 'juju', 'gris-gris', even 'diabolical', by missionary and other writers. Some anthropologists had made useful studies of particular peoples, but there seemed to be no overall description or comparison.

The study of African religion was especially difficult because there were no religious texts available. There were no written scriptures, or religious autobiographies, which might tell of belief and experience from within the religion as distinct from what might be observed from the outside. To some extent this problem remains, though the many expressions of African art can provide a kind of unwritten 'scriptures' which reveal indigenous beliefs and hopes.

I had travelled widely in the Ivory Coast in 1934-5, and now that I was back in Dahomey in 1943 there would be opportunity for fuller observation of religious practices.

* * * * *

I was sent back to Dahomey to relieve old Paul Wood and his wife and to enable them to return to France. But it had not been realized at headquarters that, with the German occupation of all France, their return would not be possible until the liberation. The Woods had heard of food shortages in France and had collected everything they possibly could to take home – locally produced soap and tinned foods sought out from shops in coastal towns and villages. They lived for months with large wooden crates filled with goods on the veranda of their seminary house. Not until the spring of 1945 were they able to get away, and meantime I had all the churches in the country to supervise, with very little petrol for travelling.

There were African ministers in charge of town churches and neighbouring villages in Porto Novo, Sakété, Cotonou, Ouidah and Anecho, and we agreed at once that they should run their own affairs and only consult me at the January synod or if there were problems. I made my headquarters up country at Dassa Zoumé, and was greatly helped in travel by my old acquaintance in the government, the Commandant Edouard Dunglas. His love of music was unabated and he often came to my Dassa house with new records, for an evening together. Dunglas had a generous petrol allowance for governmental work, and we travelled in his car over much of central and northern Dahomey developing his study of the history and religion of the old Yoruba town of Ketu. Years later I was able to publish an English version of this work through the University Press at Ibadan, Nigeria.

Earlier chapters of the present book have tried to provide some glimpses of life in Dassa Zoumé, Kilibo, and other parts of central Dahomey. Besides visiting the churches and schools, with the devoted catechists, I was able to pursue the study of aspects of Dahomean religion.

The principal traditional deity of Dassa was a goddess, Nana Buku, whose temple was halfway up the hill that overshadowed the town. Here the priestess performed her rituals, trained devotees, and gave orders to the local population. In December 1943 messengers were sent out from the temple, carrying long red poles, declaring that market prices were too high so that the poor were suffering. If prices did not fall, Nana Buku would send a plague of locusts. As locusts often appear in the dry period at the end of the year, prices dropped at once.

Travelling around Dahomey, I got to know other priests, diviners and magicians, visited temples and observed rituals, with the help of interpreters. By comparing people and places, customs and rites, with those described by other researchers in various parts of West Africa, overall comparative pictures were slowly built up.

When the Woods finally went, I became principal of the seminary at Porto Novo again, having left it five years before. New ministerial students came through from the Ivory Coast, and the growing churches required more leadership classes. The writing up of research for submission to London university for a Doctorate in Philosophy – the first, I believe, in African religion – had also to be fitted in. On the ground floor study of the house, in the evenings, with windows wide open and bats or ants flying through, the thesis was slowly typed out, entitled *West African Religion*.

* * * * *

In January 1946 a new colleague arrived from England. His French was shaky, but the students were tolerant and helpful, and I was anxious to get home as the time for my furlough had long passed the normal period. Although the war had ended the previous year, ships were still irregular, but a cable from Lagos said that one was coming and I could get a passage on it. Next day another cable cancelled the booking, but I went to Lagos all the same and got on a ship after a week.

With my chauffeur Moïse I went in the very rickety Dassa van along the new road to Lagos. The brakes hardly worked, the number plates were illegible, the tyres were worn, and we scarcely dared look under the bonnet at the engine. Over the frontier into Nigeria, driving carefully down the Lagos road, we were stopped by a burly Nigerian policeman and just managed to pull up, on the wrong side. He ran after us protesting and pulled out his notebook.

'Why you no stop? Why you go right side?' he cried.

'I am sorry,' I apologized. 'We have come from Dahomey, and you know they drive on the right there.'

'What your number? I no read it.'

He started writing in his book, and I remembered a tip I had once heard in Lagos, that the Nigerian police would never charge a missionary.

'You would not book a missionary, would you?' I queried.

'You missionary, sah?' he asked.

'Yes, from the Methodist college in Porto Novo.'

'You must make number plate clear,' he replied, putting his book away. 'Go to next village and buy some chalk to make number clear.'

We thanked him, shook hands, and went on reflecting on a justification for missions from an ordinary policeman. We got some chalk and made nice numbers on the black plates. In Lagos we went at once to a garage and thankfully left the van for repairs, with the chauffeur supervising. We said goodbye, remembering many adventures together.

Arrived in London, the thesis was duly presented to the university and passed for the Ph.D. The examiners were Professor E. O. James, doyen of religious studies, and the East African Methodist missionary-anthropologist, Edwin Smith, and both gave encouragement for further study and writing. Edwin Smith invited me to his home at Deal in Kent, in a former coastguard's house overlooking the English Channel. His library was full of books on Africa, and at his death in 1957 his collection was sent to the university library at Ibadan.

In the years after the war there was a shortage of paper, and it took three years for the thesis on West African Religion to be published by the Epworth Press. Needing to stay in Britain because of a growing family, I had been sent to the Guernsey French circuit, having been in French West Africa. But in the third year advertisements appeared of academic posts created in the new University College of Ibadan, Nigeria. My book was printed just in time and it was on the table at the interview for the first lectureship in religious studies at Ibadan, to which I was appointed. So for nine years, from 1949, I worked in Nigeria and, apart from a brief visit at the end, experiences of Dahomey had ended.

The previous pages have all been about Dahomey (now Bénin), 'the belly of the snake'. It is still a little known and generally neglected country, and these accounts are intended to provide and preserve sketches of life in that far off country in the thirties and forties of the last century. Going to Nigeria, and getting to know it far beyond the brief trips through Lagos, was quite another story.